I Lived a Dream:
My Canadian Heroes

Derek Abdul Salick

Copyright © 2016 by Derek Abdul Salick
All rights reserved. This book or any portion thereof
may not be reproduced or used in any manner whatsoever
without the express written permission of the author,
except in the case of brief quotations embodied in critical reviews and
certain other noncommercial uses permitted by copyright law.

Printed in the USA
First Printing, 2016

Derek Abdul Salick
4700 Keele St.
#11 York Lanes
P.O. Box 30311
Toronto, Ontario, M3J 2C1
Canada

www.dasalick.com

This work is dedicated to the members of the RCR family as well as their wives and children, past and present. Simultaneously, a deep appreciation for those who have fallen. Also the soldiers that suffer from PTSD and physical disabilities.

This is an attempt to recognize their hard work, loyalty, and commitment to Canada, the greatest multi-cultural nation in the world.

Let us remember them, because they are demigods; they are Canadian Heroes.

Pro Patria.

Table of Contents

Acknowledgements	vi
Infantry (A Poem)	vii
Prologue	1
Preface: Dr. Paul Brienza	3
Foreword: Dr. Livy Visano	4
THE DIALECTICS OF EMPOWERMENT	4
MITIGATING THE MILITARY	6
THE MESSAGE IN THE METHOD	10
Introduction	12
Chapter 1: Trinidad	15
Mrs. Campbell Remembers...	22
Salick Continues...	23
Welcome to Canada...The Promise Land	28
Vernon "Billy" Wilkinson	30
My New Family	34
Pte. Soulliere remembers...	35
Salick Continues...	36
Chapter 2: The Cold War	40
Cyprus	52
Dean Salick (brother):	60
The Role of the Reserves	71
Nathan Ferguson	73
Pte. Adyanga	77
Corporal Salick	82
Chapter 3: Bosnia	84
Understanding Bosnia	90
My Humanity	100
The Impact of Conflict	104
SFOR and the UN/NATO Intervention	106
Patrols	110

Private Richard Moreno:	*113*
Corporal Ben Browne/Slick 1998	*115*
From Hostility to Peace Through Football	*117*
2001	*119*
Macedonia 2001	*123*

Chapter 4: Rape as Psychological Warfare — **128**
- *Mujin* — *136*
- *Theories of Wartime Rape* — *139*
- *Feminist Ethics of Intervention* — *143*

Chapter 5: Peacekeeping — **146**
- *What are peacekeepers, and what do they do?* — *148*
- *My Heroes, Gone but Not Forgotten* — *151*
- *Robert Hodgson* — *152*
- *Robert Short* — *156*
- *Chuck Barnsley* — *160*
- *Eric Gendron* — *163*
- *My brothers who stood on guard with me, and are still here:* — *167*
- *Cory/Ricky/Ali* — *168*
- *A New Beginning* — *172*

Epilogue: Professor K. Atkinson (York University) — **173**

References — **179**

About the Author — **185**

ACKNOWLEDGEMENTS

Firstly, I would like to thank Kevin Dowdy. He insisted that I write this story because he believed it is a story for new and old Canadians alike. I would like to thank Kevin Greig, my Scottish Canadian brother who brought me back to life. Because of him, I have been contributing to the local and global communities since 1987.

I would like to acknowledge the soldiers and family members of the fallen that supported me on this journey with their stories. Also those who always gave me positive feedback and who continued to inspire me to complete this project; Wayne Evans, Paul Soulliere, Kevin Philips, Vijay Seeloch, Big Ben Brown, Sean Bohrson, Richard Moreno, Plocica, Brian Saulnier, Daniel Ruest, Onek Adyanga, Nathan Ferguson, Mrs. Sherril Hodgson and Mr. and Mrs. Gendron.

Furthermore, a huge thank you goes out to Dr. Livy Visano, Dr. Paul Brienza, Dr. Andreas Georgiou, Prof. Kirk Atkinso, and James O'Hearn for their continuous support; beginning with the publication of my first book to my current one. A special thank you to Dr. Sirvan Karimi and Dr. Mahmood Khoshchereh who also guided this project.

I would like to thank Dr. Jean Campbell for her support beginning at age 13 in Trinidad. She has continuously supported me in moving forward with my goals and ambitions. I would also like to thank my brother Dean who contributed to this book with his remembrance of us growing up on the plantation in Trinidad and our tour to Cyprus.

I would also like to thank Shawn Alli, Grant Hutchinson, Kym Santiago and Lisa Franke for their technical and administrative support.

I would like to thank the staff of Second Cup and Great Canadian Bagel at York Lanes, York University who continuously supported my projects with their kindness.

I would like to acknowledge, with gratitude, the publisher Create Space, for the courage and conviction demonstrated in promoting and publishing a subject that is replete with controversy- a story that warrants public attention.

Finally, I would like to thank the students at York university who supported me throughout the project with their kindness.

INFANTRY (A POEM)

Infantry, you have made me so proud.
You have taught me
Tolerance
Discipline and respect.
So long as I can
Keep up
With you.
Infantry,
You and I will never part.
We are the first to serve,
When our country beckons.
We will never ask why,
We will just act upon
Our duties,
Without, remorse.
Infantry, you and I,
Will stalk in the
Silence of the night.
We will run down hills
And up hills,
In the scorching sun,
In many rainstorms,
Many blizzards.
We will not stop until our
Task is done.
We will crawl on our stomachs,
Night and day.
As a team, we stand pain
that is unimaginable.
Infantry, I was once unimportant.
When I walk alongside you,
The world looks in,
And hopes to be
What you made me.
Infantry, I know I will fall Sometime,
For it is impossible to keep

up with you.
And when I fall,
There will be
sadness within me;
Along with a silent joy,
For I gave you my best,
All that I had.
Infantry, you and I,
We are not aggressors,
but keepers of peace.
Infantry, you are the most
Powerful,
Most excellent.
You rule the land.
I am truly, truly, happy, to have met you.
Infantry, you will never die. Forever, you will live.

PROLOGUE

"There is no life like it. There is no life in it." Anonymous

"When we joined, they never explained to us what could have happened. You experience it, live through it, you asked me if you did enough. Well my brother, it's like the poem says, 'You did your time in hell'." Soulliere to Salick

To Socrates, being a citizen meant being willing to give one's life for the state, to be someone who would willingly choose death over political exile. The gratitude he felt for the state was so great that even the state's desire to condemn him to death could not shake this belief. Socrates' commitment to this moral standard defined the highest expression of citizenship, a willingness to die for the state, even by its own decree. Citizenship is a privilege, one that also involves great responsibilities.

Breaking from the norm, and following one's own path is often difficult. Culture, society, and mainstream institutions often discourage this. In my own life, I have continually come across, and have been adversely affected by, dominant ideologies of race and ethnicity, and yet, while I understand and agree with the prevailing criticisms of these ideologies (colonialism, historical racism, etc), my own perspective differs.

As my life as a soldier began to wind down, I looked to study and scholarship to find answers to questions that had been growing in the back of my mind for many years. As time passed, and my studies progressed, I found that more often than not, the intellectuals I spoke with, and the scholars and journalists I read, all had one thing in common – there were a few things missing. Variables that, invariably, were curiously omitted from the discourse.

Duty, commitment, nationhood, and good citizenship. These where the guiding principles that motivated the many thousands of Canadians with whom I served. All were examples of commitment, duty, and solidarity that extended beyond race and its apologetic consequences, pushing past the racialized and criminalized "other" as excuses for youth offences, immigrant social service abuses, and criminalization in general.

There are many reasons why a soldier might enlist in the infantry, including family tradition, adventure, a desire for service, and, more often than not, economic hardship. Personally, I was originally driven by a wish for adventure, a desire that, over time, transformed into a commitment to service, to the ultimate act of citizenship that being a soldier entails.

We the soldiers never question the missions that we are asked to go on because the majority elected the government, believing that it will make the best decisions for Canada's international relations agenda.

In my opinion, we live in the greatest multicultural nation in the world. We continue to move forward by inviting in 250,000 new Canadians every year. This nation continues to set an example for global humanity, with respect for human rights, and equality.

Throughout this book, using my own life's journey as an example, I want to illustrate a way of living life beyond race, where the values of duty, nationhood, commitment, and brotherhood, are embraced as a life's guiding ethos.

PREFACE: DR. PAUL BRIENZA

What makes a hero in the modern age? This is the question raised by Salick's work. It is a question that has dominated his life, from the time of his move to Canada as a young immigrant to his distinguished service for his adopted country. It is what called him to service for his new nation and it is what has guided his post-military career. Both in and out of the military Salick has been guided by the desire to *live the life of hero* in thought and deed.

One of the oldest meanings of the word "hero" can be traced to a root that talks of protection and service to others. The hero has, in a modern world full of violent imagery, too often been associated with the one capable of aggression for the sake of a cause or country. But Salick is not satisfied with that limited view of heroism. The hero to him, and his story is a testament to this notion, is the one who protects, serves and, if the occasion calls for it, sacrifices. The hero is not only found in the thunder of battle but also in the quiet moments of compassion, care and openness. For Salick, the hero is the one who gives up what is often most important for the sake of others.

Even there, the depth of heroic character does not end. The hero is also the one who struggles with himself and with the demons of fear, ignorance and limitation. The great heroes of the Greek world, such as Odysseus, Achilles, Heracles and Oedipus, were characters that struggled with their own sense of self. That means that they were never satisfied with their own self-awareness and self-knowledge. They pushed that self-knowledge further, even when such an endeavor only served to cause pain and suffering. Socrates argued that the "unexamined life is not worth living." That phrase and the idea it expresses may be used as a moniker for the hero. The hero pushes his own understanding, the hero demands more from himself, and the hero is never complacent. In an age of egoism and self-indulgence in which the fame of a social media moment dominates the desires of many, it might be appropriate to re-examine ourselves and our sense of what a hero is. Self-indulgent ages need heroes and Salick provides us with some examples. He tells us stories of sacrifice, compassion and love of country. By love of country, Salick does not mean an unquestioning acceptance of 'my country above all else' but a critical self-examination and an understanding that we must always first be heroes in our own soul. By doing that, we may then become heroes of relevance to our families, friends, and yes, nation.

Foreword: Dr. Livy Visano

THE DIALECTICS OF EMPOWERMENT

From the Horrors of War to the Emergence of the Collective Conscientization

A country reveals itself not by its accomplishments alone, but by the events it remembers and the individuals it honors. Salick's study is a reminder of the distance still to be travelled especially as a society pulls together to expand its collective consciousness about the ravages of war and the transcendence of the spirit of hope. War reveals atrocities but often conceals the heroic and forgotten strengths of individuals. Amidst the material rubble, beneath the chaos of recovery, behind the bombastic jingoism, to the intrepid analyst there is a hitherto unrecognized authentic empowerment. Empowerment, not the banality of idle chatter about the glories of war, will serve to focus attention on the often - ignored structures and processes of injustice. Empowerment is change that results from an authentic commitment to challenge one's being, beliefs and behaviour – one's self.

Admittedly, any study of soldiering is a formidable inquiry into confrontations with conventional cultural narratives of coercion. This enterprise is a forthright interrogation of how one interprets both the familiar and the foreign; that is, how one transforms the familiar into the foreign and the foreign into the familiar. This self-study analyzes one's being reflexively in light of the pressing situational influences of one's peers. In so doing, the journey into Salick's personal experiences examines the impact of layered carceral contexts of culture and political economy on consciousness, individual and institutional. Moving beyond romanticized or demonized popular depictions of the military, fuelled by distorted profit driven corporate media sensationalism, the following discussion proffers a different set of perspectival and substantive materials; that is, a more critical selective rendering of the assortment of different "facts." First, a word of caution, Salick's expedition is replete with controversy. To the threatened, these questions will be easily discarded as rancorously polemical, rhetorically provocative and ideologically problematic. Salick's intrapsychic and intersubjective forays into the military are formidable instruments of inspiration oriented to self- growth. This intertextuality is a process whereby one text (self) plays upon other texts (fellow soldiers) endlessly to further discourses and open up the possibilities of becoming other texts.

Soldiers do not operate in isolation from wider communities in solving problems especially since the military exists within wider cultural contexts, political mediations and legal articulations. Theoretically, the soldier is an active agent situated within wider constituting contexts of social control. As a cultural subject within discourses of power, he or she is engaged in micro-political (local) struggles shaped by more macro-cultural influences (global). Militarization, as a political process and a politicized structure, enjoys a plurality of meanings that are displaced and re-constructed in concert with other hegemonic reproductions of discipline. Regrettably, militarism has become connected to alarmingly exploitative slogans designed to seduce an already impressionable audience into supporting narrow political interests.

MITIGATING THE MILITARY

The concept of the military exists as a discoursal practice that is socially or relationally situated. In addition to the state's ideological affiliation with liberalism, capitalism and modernity, the military is simultaneously institutionally linked to situationally relevant contextual codes that frame decision points or procedural judgements. The occupational/ institutional culture is one of the most significant influences on socio- conditioning that translates the spirit of soldiering. Soldiers exists in the "office" of various agencies or as often put by incumbents, it's part of the job description but it's never written down anywhere. Admittedly, officials act, not organizations per se, but officials act out of perception of organizational needs and goals (Gouldner, 1961: 87). To cope with the contradictions in both the law and organizational regulations, all agents of the military rely on the informal rules of the career culture. This culture refers to an organized and recognized constellation of values that are specific to the required activities. First, the collegium exerts influence in perpetuating a sense of professionalism replete with norms, roles and attitudes. This culture as a historically transmitted pattern of symbolic meanings communicates, perpetuates, and develops "useful" knowledge about and attitudes towards work and their "subjects." It is important to know how these agents, as representatives of a military culture, make sense of contradictions and controversy, the inscription of dominant ideologies (narratives), and, their 'preferred," "oppositional" and "negotiated" styles.

The structure of the military is a contingency that shapes the neophite's self-image, as well as his or her understanding of situational difficulties. This culture or opportunity structure awaits the arrival of prospective members. These soldiers offer both limitations to, and possibilities for, effective, critically responsive approaches. The self-identities that they construct for themselves are congruent with the possible identities that are afforded them within the professional/occupational culture. This culture provides a coherent narrative of identities, ensures social recognition of these identities and a sense of "we-ness" that stress the similarities or shared attributes around which group members coalesce. A collective wisdom emerges that serves to guide and validate perspectives and activities; normative self- serving and self -important attributes and images emerge to essentialize identity. Acculturation, that is, the process of learning the "ways and means" (coping strategies: accommodation and resistance) from collegial involvement, offers a collective solution to actual and perceived strains and values a symbolic framework for the development and maintenance of a collective identity as well as individual self-esteem.

The military, as one of the state's primary resources of power, filters trouble, funnels interpretations and marginalizes differences according to convoluted experiences and "inoculated reflexivities" (Giddens, 1992: 3) of a variety of complementary and competing ideologies. The military as the narrow reading of control is objectified according to a limited range of self-serving organizational criteria. The range of discourses used to construct this system of control consists of ideological practices that typically articulate official formations of truth. To sustain the subtext of privilege, there is no integrated text of military therein, only fragmented hierarchical canons that depict the command structure as a rational and moral authority. Authority benefits from a multiplicity of deferring signifiers that resist and inscribe narrational discourses. This manipulated corpus of essentializing customs and self-serving institutional proscriptions solely respond to "official" meanings of challenge, defined as distance and difference. Moreover, this slippage or elasticity of "deterritorialized" meanings in the military "subverts the subject" (Derrida, 1981; Lacan, 1977) by a chain of signifiers -- definitions, written and symbolic.

Caught up in the legal labyrinth of images and rituals as a priori conditioning, the military symbolizes differential identities and experiences (individual and communal) that reflect, enable, and constrain cultural meanings and realities inherent in diverse and dynamic encounters. Meanings and symbols of order penetrate permeable systems of language and individual consciousness, thereby transforming the agent-subject into a self-subordinating object. As the military monopolizes the means of mental production, the vulnerability and credulity of the individual are heightened. In this process of deconstructing and reconstructing meaning, discourses are constructed that legitimate conceptions of law in the interests of the chain of command.

Regrettably, too much attention on the military has been focused on a "mission" mandate which limits an appreciation of other equally significant roles notably fidelity or mutual reliance. Another troubling feature of conventional approaches is the glaring absence of any conceptual grasp of both the intersections of identity, institutions and ideologies and the co-joint elements in the ideological-institutional nexus. The power of this ethnographic account resides in its continual deferral of meaning (Derrida, 1981) to achieve an unmediated authorial knowledge that explains "loyalty" to the present. This poignant, well informed, balanced and compelling presentation of traditional and contemporary theoretical concerns confronts critically the celebration of the self as an agent of hope. This highly accessible book approaches eloquently competing and complementary approaches that guide the ideological and institutional constitutions of the infantry by journeying beyond the academic issues to implicate praxis and policy concerns, emphases which will provide some fascinating classroom discussions. Briefly, this book is a powerful engagement that finally moves research on the military men and women well beyond its ethnocentric borders towards a more inclusionary framework of comparative and interdisciplinary thought. Further, this text moves beyond prevailing normative claims by investigating conceptually the reproduction of the other non-visible "self" – the conferred heroism. Thus this story implicates social, political and economic struggles that reflect fundamental issues of inequality. That is, institutional forms of socialization are examined in terms of their respective relationship(s) with the state, political economy, law and culture. The acting subjects and subjected actors, within the cultural calculus, are linked to hegemonic practices. Individually and collectively the chapters enrich our conceptual appreciation of the dynamics of conflict and contribute to an understanding of generic processes that extend beyond the specific contexts of militarism. That is, this narrative demonstrates vividly how creativity pushes the field forward by interrogating privilege, deference to authority, and the arrogant imputations of dangerous defiance.

The thought provoking and stimulating chapters, provide a solid contribution to critical thought and research by addressing pervasive mediations of prevailing ideologies, unravelled within significant interactions, social organizations and social structures. In an effort to address and enlighten these issues the author has constructed an engagement with the much coherent themes of intersectionality that elucidate as well as resolve a number of thorny issues which to date have obfuscated theoretical integration. Salick presents a compelling and innovative approach to the use of professions as a resource for the production of consensus, professions as contested terrains and professions as ideological processes. The arguments are well articulated within a plethora of themes based on social location, hybridity, cross cultural communication, narratives of ideological climates and the mediations of culture and professional organizations which together create a system of meanings or moral/ control narratives. Professions, defined by dominant discourses, determine thought, affect, enjoyment, meaning and identity and various exigencies. The sensitivity to details of interpretations is a refined one and it enables readers to yield some very significant insights and to open up a key of contemporary theorization in a potentially far - reaching way. Professions in the military are socially constituted complex sets of mediations, that interconnect consciousness and society, culture and economy. I thus welcome this analysis as a novel attempt to demonstrate the character of a neglected subject by illuminating the enduring and complex influences on the informal decision making practices of professionals. This book challenges the congested closures of conventional canons characteristic of so many mainstream approaches to the military. I congratulate Salick's efforts for defying the defining gaze of professional authority and for overcoming the debilitating ethnocentrism that ignores universal inequalities of class, sexual orientation, race and gender.

Lastly, consciousness raising is emancipatory, allowing for the flexibility of thinking and listening to ourselves rather than conveniently engaging in the mindless but convenient "stir and mix" of opinions. One's self knowledge is contingent upon the available stock of information and the relevant socialization, differentially rooted cultural contexts, and the interplay of different experiences and resonating problematics. These contingencies become that much more profound in reference to class, gender, sexuality and race. The reader seeking to move outside of his or her comfort zone, to challenge his or her socialized understandings of "criminal" and "justice" in the search for the authentic, is invited to consider the contributions offered here in terms of method and message.

THE MESSAGE IN THE METHOD

Critical inquiry consists of what is said (the message) together with how it is being said (the method). It is precisely a concern for the latter that sets this experimental and experiential project apart from other investigations. The strengths of this book rest not on any one person but in the collective representation of different voices and the different forms of (re)presentations. Collectively the voices herein demonstrate courage to be vulnerable, open and challenging—to move beyond and outside of the self. The strengths of their contributions are in the connections with the subject from so many vantage points— especially race, gender, class and rank/status. The strengths derive equally from the authentic style of presentation—spontaneous, exciting and passionate. In this way, the voices offer a very rare, refreshing and empowering set of analytic tools with which to approach military service.

Obviously, no one book can hope to do justice neither to the enormous breadth nor to the depth of soldiering nor to the variety of methods available to communicate ideas. Simply to catalogue salient directions is itself an ambitious enterprise that risks trying to do too much and accomplishing relatively little. Nevertheless, this collection does offer a considerable range and variety of treatments of a variety of institutions from a refreshing mix of constituent perspectives.

I maintain that the message as well as the methods of this study is deliberately oppositional. The author in his own way and his own style challenges disciplinary canons and the totalizing view of traditional "common sense." The uniqueness of this project conceptually and methodologically exists in the different voices (tone and tenor) of the contributors.

Collectively, these voices powerfully highlight the essential elements of critical inquiry, including:

    a) a commitment and conviction to fundamental loyalty, eschewing the convenience of meanings and measurements;
    b) a courage to comprehend contradictions and dialectics (collusions and collisions) and to attempt to suspend that which has been internalized as "common" sense;
    c) a curiosity that examines the intersectionality of ideological and institutional, the immanent and transcendent;

d) a series of connections to the community (praxis) and a relatedness to interdisciplinarity; and,
e) a strength of character to be a stranger in questioning that which is presented as knowledge (culturally pervasive erasures) and moving towards an enlightened self/ social interests.

Given Salick's commitment to critical pedagogy, the criteria used to evaluate the merits of this project and its constituent contributions are broad, "outside the mainstream box" and intrinsically sensitive to those voices that have traditionally been excluded—especially those deceased, injured or forgotten. Thus, to retain the full essence of the message, editing was kept to an absolute minimum.

In understanding how the life world of soldiers intersect with the dominant practices of society, we are asked to escape from the dark and yet comfortable cave of ready-made opinions which continue to judge differences, colonize compliance and shackle the imagination. But how then does one appreciate the conditions and consequences of soldiering? The answer rests with consciousness, knowing the self and its location. First, soldiers must be understood in their own language, a style of intrinsic tension, which is dialectical in form and content. Second, the proliferation of current projects provides too much reductionism that fails to transcend local organizational politics to consider the relatedness of silencing, exclusion and inequality. Relatedness is the synthetic convergence of diverse perspectives which contributes enormously to transforming the cycle of violence. Selfhood is located culturally and remains a process of becoming.

On the one hand, Salick succeeds as a peaceful force in liberating the imagination, memory and emotions in order to realize the maturation of dreams. Accordingly, this book transcends the given and develops the complexity of being human; which involves knowing and making sense of Canada's unknown, unrepresented and unrecognized – its soldiers.

INTRODUCTION

"War is never justified, nor honourable"

- P. K. Aaron

"Each Warrior wants to leave the mark of his will, his signature, on important acts he touches. This is not the voice of ego but of the human spirit, rising up and declaring that it has something to contribute to the solution of the hardest problems, no matter how vexing!"

- Pat Riley

Marked on the body of the soldier is the whole world with its crises, abuses, developments, freedoms and peace. There are horrifying, dramatic experiences that the world has witnessed and participated in, either actively or passively. As I journey forward in life, I look back at my life, and the lives of my own personal heroes, the life we lived, and the life that some of us died for. A life I would willfully and joyously live again and again.

Imagine knowing you could die at any moment. Driving along, a bomb explodes, blowing you and your companions to pieces. Imagine wondering, everyday of your life, if you've done your duty to yourself and to others. Imagine duty and service forcing you to be a passive observer to rape, genocide, racism, ethnic cleansing, bound by military orders and hierarchical control.

This book is the engagement and struggle of a personal journey with the Canadian Army during the period of peacekeeping between the decades of 1982 to 2002. My story is not just my story, but the story of many other voices who also speak through it, as they reveal their lives and dreams through my own. I engage in a subjective historical experience that attempts an understanding of complex issues, and ideologies. An ethnography that encourages an awareness that does not refer to social or cultural paralysis.

Briefly, the structure of the books is as follows:

> Chapter 1 is focused on my journey from Trinidad, and attempts to give a background of social marginalization, racism, class, poverty and the everyday struggle for basic rights, needs and existence.

Chapter 2 provides an overview of the development, and an introduction to the Cold War, where I point out, that while Canada's role in combat in the Cold War was limited, its contributions to international peacekeeping and place in the world cannot be overlooked.

Chapter 3 explores and describes my experiences in Bosnia 1998, 2001, and Macedonia 2001. Also, I critique various moral and philosophical arguments both for and against war and go on to consider the question of a "just war."

Chapter 4 focuses on "rape as psychological warfare" in the Bosnian war, including the rape of my little 10-year-old orphan friend Tanija, an atrocity that touched the very core of my soul, which I will never forget until I die.

Chapter 5 begins with a discussion of the nature and role of peacekeeping, the history and effects of the Bosnian conflict, and how the intervention in Bosnia was key in achieving stability, peace, and hope in Bosnia today.

Many people have asked why I would fight for Canada as a new immigrant, and my reply has always been that Canada has offered me opportunities I never had in the country of my birth. The idea of fighting or standing on guard for those who cannot defend themselves has always been part of my development at a young age. The military provided me with that opportunity. Mind you, the media played on my mind in a great way in the defense of freedom, human rights, equality for ethnic groups, women, and according to Pierre Trudeau (RIP), *"it does not matter what you do in your bedroom with who, so long as you are a progressive minded individual."* The values of this nation were something worth defending.

When I speak of my own personal heroes, soldiers I served with, whose thoughts and deeds have altered the course of my own life, I refer to them as demigods, as an act of remembrance, honour and worship. These Olympians, who I had the fortune and pleasure of calling my comrades, are the bones and body of this humble work.

Throughout history many others have lived with "haros" (death), and have danced and made friends with the devil. However, very few have lived, fought, and died as heroes, as demigods, as my boys have, and I believe that this narrative will do my brothers a measure of justice as it would the many other fallen soldiers of the RCR family. I believe that, in time others will join me in celebrating these brave souls who have fallen for the idea of a more "just world." I called them, and still see them as "my Heroes." They stood on guard for me throughout some of the most horrible experiences of my life. Let these noble souls remind us of some of the pillars of virtue Canada was founded on. To these brave servants of the peace and stability that we call the free world order, I dedicate what follows.

Chapter 1: Trinidad

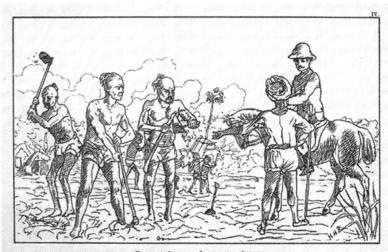

(Tenneh) Digging Lands for Indigo

I was born on an island paradise in the Caribbean Sea, geographically located next to Venezuela. Trinidad and Tobago, my original home, is a nation that is full of life, colour, and fun. Often seen as a Caribbean version of Canada, in that it is a democratic, multi-ethnic post-colonial nation, Trinidad and Tobago has a dark side that is often overlooked. The nation has long been torn by racial discord, having seen numerous armed insurrections, and has constantly been plagued by racially charged politics since achieving full independence in 1962.

I was born of a mixed race, African-Aboriginal and South Asian, what is known as the Dougla ethnic group. It is interesting that, given the intensity of their dislike for each one another, the "Dougla identity" was forged from intermarriages, and other kinds of liaisons between South Asians, Aboriginals, and (black) Africans. This meant that their offspring inherited a virtual "double dose" of negative self-identity: for instance, in Trinidad and Tobago, it is common knowledge that the "Dougla mix" are the least privileged people in society, and are placed invariably at the bottom of the social spectrum. Two major reasons for this is that once an African and South Asian person became involved in a relationship, the offspring was usually considered a "bastard" child, similar to being the child of a prostitute. When one considers the derivation of the term "Dougla," it is racist, socially destructive, and very discriminatory.

As a Dougla, I was given up for adoption at an early age because when an African and South Asian came together in Trinidadian society, the South Asian family often disowns the member who "shamed" the family by coupling with a member of another race. But in a land where men are expected to get two to three women pregnant to prove their masculinity, it is a recipe for disaster, leading to any number of fractured families, and outcast Dougla children.

My father is an example of this mentality, as he had a few women with children. It appears to be normal with a high percentage of Trinidadian men. They lacked responsibility, and when the families did not have a strong economic base, the children were often left behind. Racial politics did not help the situation either. Finally, the lack of equality for women in a patriarchal post-colonial society made it difficult for women to fend for themselves, or their children, with the lack of rights and stable family environments.

I remember living with my adopted family. We would pitch marbles, and play Cowboys and Indians. Although I was always the 'Red Indian,' it did not occur to me that life was not good. I saw children of different ethnic backgrounds playing in the school yard, not being affected by race or class. When we attended Sunday school, the Preacher would say to us, "If you are suffering and poor you must always pray to Jesus Christ because he will come and save us, yes he will" and, "The meek shall inherit the Earth one day." For a while, I believed him. But then I met reality.

I was eight when my first adoptive mother died. I remember going to the funeral as they lowered the coffin into the ground. People all around me were screaming, crying and shouting. As the coffin was lowered, I picked up a handful of soil and threw it on top. I did not fully understand what happened. I didn't understand death, and I didn't cry. All I could think, however, was when my adopted mother was alive, where were all those people?

After the funeral, there was now confusion about what would happen to the Dougla (me). My adoptive father, brother, and sisters were silent. That very night at the house I heard someone say that my "father" would be coming to take me away. They didn't have to worry about the Dougla any more.

I'll never forget meeting my father. At around 8pm, a man walked in, half-drunk, red in complexion, 6 feet tall, and strong in his appearance, and said to me '*son go pack your things.*' '*What things?*' was all I could think. All my possessions in the world amounted to two pairs of shorts and two t-shirts.

I said good bye to my adopted brothers and sisters, very briefly, with few words spoken, and then I was walking down the hill with my drunken father. As we were walking, he told me how good his family would treat me, and that I had an uncle in England!

'*What a big family I belong to,*' I thought. But after entering St. James, and visiting the homes of relatives, I learned that I did not have a family after all. They literally refused to accept me. But my father was undeterred. And told me that he would take me to see Aunt Wendy, who was a 'Red Creole Lady.' She was actually not a relation, only an "aunt" in the sense that all adults are called "aunt" or "uncle" in Trinidad, similar to how this occurs in South Asian societies. Unsurprisingly, "Aunt" Wendy did not want me either. Perhaps my father thought she would be swayed by my Dougla nature, and would see me as of her kind. To Aunt Wendy's credit, she let us stay the night.

The next morning we were up at six, and off to see two of my brothers. Although I haven't mentioned it yet, I was the third of five siblings, with three brothers and a sister. In my later years I would add four more half-siblings to this total, on account of my father's further adventures in siring offspring.

Though it is often joked that the middle child is the forgotten child, in my case I literally was forgotten, given up, thrown away. That morning after leaving Aunt Wendy's, we headed east towards Barataria where I met my two brothers who were working on an agricultural plantation.

One was seven and the other was nine. It was the first time I had met them in my life. Strangely, to this day, the thing I remember most was that I did not have a toothbrush that day, and instead I took the leaves on a branch and some salt and brushed my teeth as we walked. I wanted to be my best possible self when I met my brothers.

I became part of that family for five years, with me and my brothers working all hours of the day in order to earn a roof over our heads and three square meals a day. The plantation life was not the most pleasant life for children at our age, but it was either that or die of hunger. I could have been resentful for the situation I was in, but I wasn't. Those five years served as a lesson to me, allowing me to have an understanding of capitalism in that period where labour is exploited to the maximum. This family did not have to take me in, but they did, and I will always be grateful for that.

Although the plantation life looks a lot like slavery, I was never a slave. It was, however, a form of indentureship. We were up at 6am, and on the plantation for 6:30am. We would cut the big bush, create bundles and burn them while we continued cutting the big bush, one acre at a time. As we completed one acre, the tractor would come and turn up the soil. We would then make banks to plant the seed, and simultaneously we would dig drains for proper irrigation. In the rain season we could not afford to allow the land that the crops were on, to be waterlogged. Thereafter, we would plant acres of the seed of certain crops, such as tomatoes, cabbage, and cauliflower. Thereafter we would do half acres of celery, lettuce and pak choi. Throughout this we would have to water the crops three times a day, starting at 7am, then 1am, and finally at 5pm. By 7pm we would be in our homes for our evening meal. This was my life, day in day out. There was no space for dreams, only space for basic survival.

Another must-do task was preparing all the goods for the market in Port of Spain or the San Juan market. We would pile lettuce, celery, tomatoes, cabbage, cauliflower, and cucumber in a truck headed for the Port of Spain market. Often we were hoping to meet a middle man, who would purchase most, or all of the goods, so we could head home early. Otherwise I would be pushing a wooden box wheel barrow on Friday and Saturday evening, through the community, selling food crops. Saturday and Sunday morning, I would be pushing the very same wheel barrow to the San Juan market once again to sell the aforementioned produce. Sometimes my brothers would accompany me, but more often than not I would do it alone.

During this period of my life, I often endured racial abuse. At time, my brothers and I had to fight to defend ourselves. For example, one evening while walking to the family house from the north to the south, eight young South Asian boys ambushed us and started beating us with sticks. Bruised and beaten, we ran away. Upon reaching the household, we told the plantation owner what had happened. In response, he did not go out to find those South Asian boys to punish them. He punished us, because we ran away, thereby bringing shame to his house.

Our punishment was to kneel on graters, holding a rock in each hand, facing the wall and then flogged with a leather belt soaked in cow urine. The next morning while we were still in the punishment position, one of the young men was passing by and laughing because we were punished. My brothers and I dropped the rocks and beat that boy like a 'Good Friday Bobolee' (Bobolee is a version of the beating of Judas on Good Friday in the Caribbean).

His parents came over to the house to make peace with the plantation owners. They wanted no more violence. However this was a physical peace only. The verbal abuse continued, and never stopped.

Later in life, when I had a chance to speak to my younger brother Dean about this time, he asked me if I remembered when I had first arrived at Barataria, when he and my older brother Dexter (Rest in Peace) would tie my hands behind my back, and beat me. They had to "tame me," he said, because I looked like a wild savage.

In the late 1960's and early 1970's, the government began buying land from the plantation owners, and the need for our labour decreased. At the same time, The People's National Movement's (PNM) government insisted that all young people had to attend school, which is why my brothers and I soon found ourselves sitting in a classroom, studying English, basic math, history, and, most importantly, sports.

My older brother and I played football (soccer) for our schools, and my younger brother played basketball. Meanwhile, on the plantation, there were two young brothers of African descent living with their family in a new government housing project, next to the plantation. These two young boys, Russel and Alvin Frank, would come to the plantation to assist us in doing our work so that we could finish early, and play street football beside the plantation.

Football was the great equalizer. Playing football at St. Georges College, it was the only time I could compete on an equal footing with the whites, the blacks, and the South Asians. Around that time, the Mighty Composer (a calypso singer) called me over and said "[y]oung *man, it is time for you to play cricket. I do not want to see you doing drugs, like the rest of the older boys.*" And that I did. Football and cricket created the only space for me to give my 100%, and where I would not be considered less because of my ethnic makeup. I learned to play only to win, and because of that, today, whatever challenges I am presented with, I never quit.

Looking back, it was a blessed time in my life. Even though life was hard, I was in a good spot compared to so many others on the island. Unfortunately, good things never last forever, and one Friday afternoon, after high school, football training went a bit late, and one of the plantation owner's sons decided to get physical with me, and I defended myself. Inevitably, there were consequences for doing this.

At the age of fourteen, going on fifteen, I was kicked out of the house and my world took another path. Neil Blanche, my best friend at the time, gave me twenty-five cents and a piece of Dentyne chewing gum. Besides this, all I had my school uniform, and so it was that on the advice of Neil, I headed to the bus shelter in Port of Spain. I arrived at the station about 8pm that night, and I sat on a bench.

The hours stretched, and flowed with agonizing slowness. Everywhere around me were the poor, those on cocaine, marijuana, and alcohol, it was a rude awakening, and I knew one thing was for sure - this would not be my life.

When dawn finally arrived, I decided to orient myself to the area. I walked out of the bus station taking notes of the different names of the streets, and I actually drew a footpath as I walked up and down Charlotte. Henry and Frederick street and the Savannah were as far north as I would reach, as the bus station was south of the Savannah. This would now be my home until I could find my own space, so I located a couple stand pipes so that, even if I couldn't hustle some food, I would at least have water to drink.

During that time I noticed the other people around me, seasoned hustlers who knew how to survive. Some would beg for pennies, some would steal, some would help shop owners move goods around in exchange for a small tip. My approach was very simple. I would pick up bottles and take them to shopkeepers, and in turn I would receive a penny for each bottle I turned in. Yes, life was different, but all I really needed to survive was two rock cakes a day and a red Solo Sweet drink. I was thrown into a world, where the stagnancy around me would not allow me to dream or to achieve anything. The humans around me were living like dogs, in that the bigger and meaner dog had the greater piece of the pie.

I would regularly go down to the bus station as though everything was normal. Older people would ask me what I was doing and I would reply, *"I am waiting for my mother and father."* Even though it was quite obvious I was telling a fib, the older people would still kindly say *"I hope they come and get you."*

The days and nights dragged on. At times I just wanted the night to be over so I could start the next day. All the street hustlers, the pimps, ladies of the night, drug dealers, and as the night goes on the drunks became tough and the fighting commenced, and thereafter the police would intervene.

When morning came, the working folks rushed by to commence their jobs. Seeing them move with haste and a sense of purpose, I vowed that the world I was living in would not be my world for long.

Life, at times, appeared to be strange as I sat at the bus station pondering my next move. Three months later, I decided to visit my school teacher Mrs. Campbell. Upon seeing me, she stated, *"Salick, Neil told me what happened. Boy, we have to make life better for you."*

MRS. CAMPBELL REMEMBERS...

It must be by divine intervention that I was placed as a French Teacher at St. George's College, Barataria, Trinidad & Tobago, in 1975 and was entrusted with a Grade 8 (Form 3) class of teen co-eds. A brilliant, outspoken, effervescent bunch, they were.

As I conducted my one on one interviews with them during the lunch hour, I began to understand the interesting beings that I was expected, not just to teach French, but I was being called upon to mentor and guide their energies in my capacity as Form Teacher. They were thirty-five in all, each with a different history. It was not long before I became attached to that class – Form 3R.

They all opened up to me...except one sad, surly, withdrawn student who sat at the back and during his interview, would only mumble in response to my promptings, obviously uninterested and hardly impressed.

In fact, Derek Salick became so angry at one point that he actually yelled at me as I tried to get him to off-load his problems. I had to back-off. Then he disappeared from school and could not be found.

Fast forward three months. His classmates are now in Form 4 (Grade 9), having selected the subject areas they might pursue later in life. There is a knock on the door of the Language Room where I was teaching and I open to find Derek, out of uniform but proudly wearing the St. George's College badge. He was now ready for school again.

The then acting Principal would not accept him back into school. Oh well! That was the impetus I needed. Sneak him in, find 8 teachers willing to accept him in their classes, very quietly, until we could figure things out. It was important to get him off the streets. No trouble whipping up support. Uniforms, schoolbooks and a very kind foster mother were found and then a search for Derek's parents.

SALICK CONTINUES...

That very evening, Mrs. Campbell took me to my second adopted mother's home. I got a job working as a construction labourer, making $5 dollars a day, Monday to Friday. Not Canadian or American dollars, Trinidadian dollars, which meant about $1 CDN a day, by the exchange rates of the time. Simultaneously I picked up another job pumping gas at a Pillai gas station in Maraval on the weekend days, making $3.25 a day. Then, at nights on the weekends, I worked at Bergerac hotel as a bus boy making $2 per evening.

While I was organizing myself financially, Mrs. Campbell was organising with my mothers' sister to get me to Canada, where my biological mother was living at the time. This was something that had never crossed my mind, something that I could not even imagine with my experience and limited education.

I never expected to travel to Canada, because many come to you and talk about grander spaces, and in many cases, that's all they do. Therefore, every moment, every opportunity, I lived as though it was my last. I remember after work, during the week days, I would run down the hill to play football on a gravel pitch where most of the players were older. Some would drink, smoke, and use crack cocaine, and they would say to me, "*Red Man* (or Wild Man), *we do not want to see you doing what we are doing. If you do, we will break your hands. You have an opportunity we never had, you are attending a college, and you will work for the government one day.*"

They just wanted to see me do better.

Mrs. Jean Campbell at the London Olympic Games. Mrs. Campbell became the mother I never had, a big sister, a mentor, and a lifelong friend. I hope God continues to shower her with great blessings.

At sixteen, I moved to Boissiere, where I paid a rent of $25 per month, and working at the Bergerac hotel. It was there that I learned that a little more kindness would get you better tips from tourists or wealthy Trinidadians. That summer I continued to work hard, played a lot of football, and started becoming socially and more politically aware of the class or group of people I belonged too.

Survival required hard work, but beyond that, however, where was I going? Nowhere. People like myself and my friend Neil were stuck in a rut, which is how we began to run with the Black Power movement, lead by charismatic black men who urged us to take up arms against the oppressive PNM regime.

Back then, everything seemed so clear, so black and white. However, today, upon reflection, I have to recognize and acknowledge that the late Dr. Eric Williams and his administration could only do so much when one considers that their political and economic strategies of development were still influenced by the British, in that Britain still had the final say. Therefore, the leadership was not built of magical men and women who could solve social problems with the wave of a magical wand. Trinidad went from a dependent colonial state with no established institutions of self-governance to an independent nation, pretty much over night. These conditions would not allow for a perfect society, and those who opposed the government were short sighted, unable to properly understand the developmental goals of the PNM.

In any event, when I was on the plantation, I did not understand the words *exploitation*, *oppression*, or revolution. The blacks stood up against their own Black Government in 1970 with the Black Power Movement. Later on, in 1976, there was a new awakening, I was in school and I now understood these words, they meant something to me as I observed the mighty rich in their huge homes, two and three cars in the driveway, and swimming pools in the backyard. When one has lived from hand to mouth, subsisting on scraps, and drinking out of rusty pipes at a public bus terminal, this kind of wealth was unimaginable.

On the hill where I lived, in small tin-roofed house that had seen better days, I worked seven days a week, studying at school when I could. Even though school was free, I paid for the books. I paid for travel to school, I paid to live in that old house, and paid for my food. I was proud to be able to make my own way, as there were many others around me who were much worse off, but nevertheless it burned to see these privileged elites with so very much, who did so very little, and whose only skill seemed to be knowing how to siphon the wealth of the nation into their own pockets.

Education opened my eyes to the injustices around me, such as a police force that protected the interests of the rich and the government.

Was I doomed to suffer this injustice? Though many today forget, the 70's were a tumultuous time in world history. Castro was in power in Cuba, exporting Cuban Communism throughout the region. Mao had full control of China, which was embroiled in the madness of the cultural revolution. College students would eagerly pass around dog-eared copies of the Communist Manifesto. This time marked the height of the Vietnam War, and the counter-cultural movement in the US.

I remember one Friday, when Neil and I were invited to a meeting with revolutionaries. They were a mix of Trinidadians and Cubans hoping to spark a proletariat revolution. We were in school, and we had planned our exit with military precision. As as the school bell was about to ring, just before the gate was to close and lock us into the school grounds for the day, we made our escape. But to our surprise, Mrs. Campbell appeared. "*Young men, where are you going?,*" she asked us. Neil replied that we were just going for lunch. Knowing we were up to no good, which she clearly stated to us, she arranged a lunch for us on the school grounds.

There are only a few moments in life where one can truly say, "*If not for...then.*" If not not for Mrs. Campbell stopping us from skipping school to attend a meeting with these revolutionaries, then I would most assuredly not be here today to write my story. My story would have ended on the bank of the St. Joseph's river, where the bodies of those we were to meet with were found the next day. They had been killed by the police, sold out by their own comrades in the movement.

I remember the following Monday, when Mrs. Campbell talked about the pen being mightier than the sword. My position at the time was that those words had little bearing on reality, and meant very little to me. Where was the justice? The 'Haves', will not oppose the system that gave them a comfortable life. The 'Have Nots', who fight back then ultimately fail because they lack an education and a vision.

At the time, I was young, angry, educated at the high school level and felt helpless in my position, where I was witness to injustice and inequality daily. I began to ponder how to achieve a fair and just society at the age of fifteen. Today, I have lived in or visited fifteen countries, and I have witnessed global inequalities, therefore I beg the question, as a human race, are we making progress when one considers equality and social justice?

I remember one day, later on in history class, Neil and I were sitting in the back of the classroom while our teacher lectured on Egypt and she asked the question, *"who would like to visit Egypt one day?"* All the rich or well-to-do students raised their hands, and Mrs. Melville asked, *"Salick and Blanche, how about both of you?"*

We looked at each other and laughed, because this was not something within the realm of possibility for us. We barely considered ourselves as true members of the school body, because of the social class that the majority represented.

Today I remember boys who belonged to the classless, and I remember those who I competed with every day, be it in cricket, or football, or in the classroom. I remember the likes of Gabriel Bernard who was a member of the new Dougla ethnic group. I remember as we took on the big colleges like QRC, St. Mary's, and Fatima. Gabriel and myself would bowl the opening overs, and I would specifically bowl to bruise the opposing batsmen. When we played football, we gave everything and played our hardest. We were the classless playing the fortunate. But when the game ended, and playtime was over, so was our equality, and our ability to compete.

When I was 16, my education was just beginning, but my impoverished state seemed never ending. I couldn't see any future for myself, and was losing the will to try to. Luckily for me, Mrs. Campbell did not feel the same, and had continued to work with my mother's sister, and my brothers and I were given the green light to move to Canada, for a new beginning.

WELCOME TO CANADA...THE PROMISE LAND

As you enter into Canadian air space, as you look down and observe the high-rise buildings, the city lights, it is only then that you understand how different your life is going to be. For a moment, I thought about the movies, and New York City. We were sold on the idea of "The American Dream," where the streets are lined with gold and winning was easy. As the cliché goes, I had to pinch myself as I landed in Toronto, Canada, to convince myself it was real

At the Lester Pearson airport, I met my biological mother for the first time, three days before my 17th birthday. My mother approached me and said to me 'my son, my son', and honestly it was difficult to understand those words, because I survived the harshest period of my life without her, and now her presence seemed strange to me. The years of absence from each other's life forced us into a relationship of strangers, but I was willing to give us another chance at a mother and son relationship.

Arriving at the house, I met my older sister and my youngest brother and a stepsister. My mother now had a second husband. With all the surprises, twist and turns, the focus was a better life, and to achieve that, a better education, and work to make university possible. However, the head of the household had different plans for us, and education was part of those plans. His agenda was for us to work to pay the bills, so that he could become a worthier immigrant, building his status on our backs. He was like the plantation owner I had worked for, but worse, as he did not have the interests of me or my siblings in mind in any form whatsoever.

While in Toronto I enrolled at Albert Campbell High School, and I joined the cross-country team. By the end of November that year, we moved to Oshawa and I enrolled at R. S. McLaughlin Collegiate, with my youngest brother. I found a job working as a dishwasher at $3.25 an hour from winter to spring, and in the summer I would go and work with Aldo, an Italian gentleman in construction, as a labourer being paid the princely sum of $5.00 an hour. It was hard, backbreaking work, but I developed a friendship with these Italian young men: Gino, Vince, Mauro and Joseph. We worked together Monday to Friday, and on Sundays we played football with some of my other school friends.

While at R.S. McLaughlin I ran the 400 and 800 meter for Track and Field, and felt rather honoured and privileged to have Mr. Carson Petrie as a track and field coach, who had competed for Canada internationally in the 400 meters in the 1960's. Mr. Carson would take us on weekends and train us after school. He believed in hard work, commitment, dedication and the right respectable attitude. He was truly an unbelievable human being.

My focus was on my education, and at the end of the summer I moved to Toronto where I enrolled at George S. Henry Academy. After one year in my mother's house, I went my own way. Although I would continue to keep in contact with my brother and sister, my dream of being with the family of my birth had died.

Thankfully it wouldn't be long before I discovered my true family, the family I would have for the rest of my life. But before that, I met Vernon "Billy" Wilkinson.

VERNON "BILLY" WILKINSON

I entered Canada in my early teens from Jamaica. I met you (Salick) and your brothers in early 1980 with Emmerson through his disc jockey sounds (Enchantment). We lived a care free life, we were all new immigrants and we were searching, looking for ourselves in society. In many ways we were outcasts, our understanding of the world around us was limited. What I knew our mission, was to work hard and complete our grade 12 education. We avoided the street life because it never really attracted us. We were not criminally minded. For one to achieve economic freedom, one must work hard. After school, we did odd jobs, dishwashing in the winter nights, and in the summer, the labour force on the construction sites.

I met Mike, Alex, Ronaldo, Dean, Dexter and Darren and we were all young early 20s. We drank beer, and you will drink orange juice, we cook, we eat, you know, we didn't really have much need of money other than just our basic survival,

Life was simple and we didn't have any cars or anything, we walked wherever we wanted to go. We had to work day jobs, little money here and there. And one of the most profound change that came in our life,

Remember Tony Plumber? Big black guy from England? He used to intimidate people eh? He usually walked with a pit-bull and he was deported back to England.

We were trying to finish our education at the high school level. It did not matter how difficult it was however we succeeded in the end.

Dean was the first one to go, he joined the military. That was a sign that we are changing that we were growing up and have to conform. And then you joined the military. I didn't want to go that route. At that stage of my life I was seeking another direction however, earlier on before that, I tried military but I didn't like the structure. I didn't like the idea of gunshots and drinking a lot of beer and marching around. But that was it, I personally did not like it. I think it was a great career for you. Not only a career but as a tool for transformation, the military that time was a respected institution. If you were going to the military, it meant something. Not like today, going to military is looked at negatively. It was a positive thing because the world was safer but we were made to think that is was dangerous.

It was the Cold war. We were told that the USSR was the evil empire in the east. Hence, everything was derived from those ideologies. So obviously when you go to military, you were trained that way, that you bind to that, that you are going to fight the war against Russia and eastern European allies, right?

So, you know that's basically how we were programmed to think. To see the world through the eyes of two competing ideologies which at the time those ideologies represented us. And we were supposed to hate those people who never did anything to us.

Yeah, we had no clue. But today we know that they wanted the same thing we wanted. The first time I saw you from the military, you were starting to change, you know, you looked stronger, and you were more vocal, you had stronger opinions about the world because by then you had gone to a few other places and see more of Canada than us. You know, we are basically here in Toronto, getting ready to be super programmed, you know, to become workers in the system, this is what the society does to you. You just become completely absorbent, we become functionary, you know, just to work. You don't get any chance to say anything or make any decision about anything, to have an input. You look for jobs and you go to work. If somebody tells you what to do, you get it done, and you get your pay. That's how I was living my life, you know. You're in the military you get to see things differently, you are enjoying yourself.

Salick:

The infantry was a dream to travel to far distant countries, meet new and exciting people and stand in no man's land's to defend the helpless, provide humanitarian aid where possible and contribute to global humanity. We constantly prepared for war to opposed corrupted governments that have no respect for their own citizens. They would go to the extent of selling their mothers and sisters into prostitution for economic gain. We will chase and keep war criminals away from the defenseless, those who were abused, mentally and physically, for example, rape, the innocent. I represented the Canadian military team in a few countries playing football/soccer. And this was part of an approach to create friendship, better relationship with locals and other military organizations.

The military paid me to stay fit, travel to these foreign countries to amend peace. I knew when I signed the dotted line, you live or you die. And that's it, you know. In the end I enjoyed the life.

Billy:

I mean, honestly, I know you gave up a lot for that. You're a grown man now, you don't have any kids, family, you know, the fact that I stayed here, it was very hard, it was difficult to survive and to live in the system because opportunities were so limited.

Without education or skills, you are basically nothing, you know. You're just a worker. And you know, I never had any of those things. I thought I knew things, you know I was very well literate as a person and have understanding and capabilities but opportunities were lacking and I just accepted that that was just the way it works. Live for and die for.

Now I see different. I know that there are tremendous resources and opportunities to have a good life. I also know that there is a competing force to deny him of a have a good life because there are people that want to take everything that you earn. They find different ways to steal. The government will grab you from tax. And also, people will snake us because everybody want money. They find ways to take it. They want to get rich quick by taking your money. Fraud is wrong, you know.

You always wanted to go to the military, that was what we always talked about. So when you did get to the military, it was great when you got accepted.

Yeah, you know, you always explained what your vision and life goals were in life. That you want to participate with the government. And you always thought the need of having your own ideas documented so you can bring them forward and having a book that shows that you have an understanding about the history of your country and also you have information that you can give to others. Because I think you are about educating others too, that is part of your character as a leader that you want to educate others and you want to bring others along with you. You don't want to go forward alone and you started to realize that when you build your own organization, you influence people to do good. So in order to have people believe in you, it is best to have some kind of ideas that you can put forth on the table say these are my beliefs and these are my goals that I want to achieve, you know. And to ask people question that do you want to work with me? Do you want to help me achieve? And what is your vision? You know? The other person. You are in the right track because I think becoming part of the government, you have to have a strong back bone, you know. And you have to make sure you have your ideas put together to make sure you have the strength to deal with these people because they are pretty sharp. A lot of them want to be on top, they are sharp.

MY NEW FAMILY

"To Close Within and Destroy the Enemy, In All Types of Terrain and Weather."

My entrance into the army began on an innocuous note. I was with my friends sitting outside a coffee shop at 3:00am in Oshawa, Ontario, as we were all pondering our next move in life and when we would make that move. Vince and Gino decided that they would continue with construction with their father. Tim and Joe would go to college, and Tony focused on becoming an electrician. I knew my next move was the Canadian Armed Forces as I was just waiting for my citizenship. I was also subjected to the influence of the media. I was inspired when I observed soldiers picking up arms to fight for justice and equal rights.

When I saw the biographical movie "To Hell and Back," with Audie Murphy (the most decorated American soldier of World War II, who acted in the movie), I was convinced that the military, and more specifically, the Infantry, would be my life. Although I let them know what I was planning out, the comments started for example; "Do you want to go get killed? Those commie bastards will kill you, those Nazis do not like black people, they will string you up."

On June 1st 1982, I jumped on a bus from Oshawa to Trenton.

PTE. SOULLIERE REMEMBERS...

"We were all gathering at Trenton, and you in your yellow hoodie, pinstriped dress pants and dress shoes, you were very personable; talking to everyone as if you knew them personally. Asking where they were from and what trade we were going into. Most of us were in the combat arms infantry or artillery. That flight must have been a milk run, I swear we took off and landed more times than I could count.

When we finally landed in Nova Scotia, we were ushered onto school buses for the long ride to CFB Cornwallis. We arrived at 5:00am and were ushered into a dining hall, and after a few minutes of milling around you could hear this clicking noise hitting the pavement outside the drill hill. A Sergeant entered and the yelling began, we were told to form ranks. "What?" "Form a line!" he yelled as he began pushing us into position. The rows deep as arm's length apart. He ordered us to drop our bags and open them. He wacked down each row, picking through our stuff with his pace stick. If you had so much as an Aspirin, he knocked it out of your pile of belongings with his pace stick. One guy had brought a case of beer with him. The Sergeant looked at him stunned; all the guy could do was shrug his shoulders. After his inspection, we received our first meal: breakfast. We formed up, or what we considered forming up, as the Sergeant led us to the mess hall. we marched, the rest of the base began to awaken. Out of the windows and as we passed by recruits we heard Alice. "Alice," we kind of looked at each other, "Who the hell is Alice?" All the way to the mess hall we kept hearing Alice. Like running a gauntlet, from every window in every barracks. "Alice, Alice'" They kept calling. By the time we reached the mess hall, one curious young man spoke up. "Excuse me, Sir, but who is Alice?" "First of all, don't call me Sir, I'm a Sergeant, I work for a living. And second, you're all fucking Alice!" Again, we looked at each other and we all had the same dumb expression on our faces. Why would we be called Alice? I think the Sergeant must have seen the same expression a thousand times. "It is because of your long hair; you bunch of idiots."

SALICK CONTINUES...

Later that day I was no longer "a long hair, non-dope smoking, puffy eyed, Jesus Christ Freak." My life was about to change; and that it did, forever. Initially the experience was humbling. The boys were from across Canada, which amounted to 135, At the end of twelve weeks, the numbers would drop, as many recruits did not make it through basic training. I will always remember some of those initial experiences. They were raw, unspoiled, filled with innocence really. Some of the boys had never even seen a real black or brown person up close. When Kevin Reid first looked at me, he said "Salick, can I touch you? I always saw your kind on television." My reply was simple. "Give me a hug man." At that moment I realized racism, and discrimination come about when cultures clash; and we really know so little of each other, which includes belittling stereotypes in place of real knowledge. It was a humbling moment. But, overall, when the 'ice had been broken' these first fumbling attempts to get to know each other disappeared.

Everybody, especially the infantry boys, worked for each other. 'Iron sharpening iron,' our instructors were hardcore professionals, these are the men you want to be like, men who would live and die for in the infantry world. There was Mcpl. Burke, an instructor who was a machine, he could have run forever and then some. He was also a drill God, his words of command just ripping the skies as his voice carried across a parade square. He wore the RCR cap badge on his beret.

Training was hard, the secret though, 'Never Quit'. I remember these boys like yesterday. Soulliere, Phillips, Milton, Olaski, La Belle, Leavitt, Palmer, Game, Langton, Doctor. At the end of basic training, our numbers whittled down to 97: with 30 of us going into infantry, and the rest absorbed into trades. However, by the time we were on our way to CFB Petawawa, we encountered other infantry men waiting to start their QL3; which swelled our ranks to 80 men.

The training at CFB Petawawa was infantry-specific. The words that first come to mind would describe this type of training as "hardcore." We did things that would kill regular human beings. For example, we would perform to the highest level of the four phases of war without food and water for 72 hours. This involved marching for days and nights with our full battle load with minimum rest; oftentimes we would rest 3 hours in a 24-hour period. We would also crawl on our stomachs under barbed wire while machine guns were shooting at us. It was a really fearful experience, but the boys on the left and right of you, and the section commanders, made sure you did things right so that you would not get hit from a live bullet. You placed your life in imminent danger, and laughed about it at the end. The discipline and the comradeship that we developed during these exercises were something that mere words cannot explain.

I will say this though. Including myself, my boys were united by a common idea of nationhood: strength, honour and discipline. As far as I am concerned, we were unlike the rest of Canada and the World. This is the inspired state of consciousness I was in by the time our QL3 was completed. Upon graduation, we were dispersed to different English speaking Infantry Battalions across Canada; 12 of us went to CFB Gagetown.

Post-graduation placements occurred on December 18th 1982 and we were now in our battalion, 2RCR at CFB Gagetown. We were now members of Hotel Company nicknamed, "Hollywood" Company. One would automatically think of movie stars, and yes, we were, or we felt like movie stars.

We were all placed in rifle platoons and then given a short leave to visit our families. Then, on January 7th 1983, we were selected for some more iron-sharpening-iron training which commenced with my first winter exercise in minus 30-degree temperatures, constantly training for all phases of war. This ended three weeks later.

Given a choice of toiling in a frozen wasteland, my brothers at my side, and wasting away the days on a warm Trinidadian beach, I will choose that winter exercise every time.

Paul Soulliere with 50 calibre machine gun (1983). Photo provided by SGT. Steve Young (RIP).

Next, we were assigned to QL3 courses, where I was sent on the machine gun course. It was exciting, all about firepower. I remember Sgt. Garnett calling me out.

"Pte. Slick link all the tracer rounds. You will have the last shoot."

I linked a belt of tracers with Pte. Soulliere, over 200 plus rounds. Sgt. Garnett asked, *"Private Slick are you ready and who is your number 2?"*

"Pte. Soulliere," I replied, then turned to Soulliere and said, *"I will roast the sky with tracer rounds and we will shoot down every drone."* Paul said *"Let's show these mothers what we are made off, aruh."*

After our Machine Gunners course, the Battalion "All phases of War Exercise" commenced, it was early spring. The terrain in CFB Gagetown's training area is something you cannot really prepare for. One moment we would be experiencing a snowstorm and immediately afterwards, the sun would smile down on us. Just suddenly thereafter we will have heavy showers, thunder rolling as though the devil is laughing at us and saying 'you silly fools, ha, ha,'.

Myself and Soulliere were the section support weapons team, we carried C2s and the GPMG with a few belts of automatic fire, and iun the rifle company attack, we will then be part of the Rifle Company Fire Base. This was my first real Battalion exercise, at least six hundred Infantrymen everyone in the field and everyone assigned a specific role, it was still cold early spring unbelievable weather. It was cold and wet, snow, heavy rain, mud, and the days in between God will smile with us and give us a beautiful sunshine. In our rucksacks we had our wardrobe, our sleeping kit with our personnel bivouac bags and seventy-two hours of rations/food. In our duffle bags we had extra kit just in case of emergencies. I thought to myself 'what a life'? There isn't any other place I will rather be. These Soldiers are a special breed of human beings, they are modern day demigods. This was a test of one's true desire to be an infantryman, the terrain, the hardness demonstrated by our leaders; Sgt. Desmond, Mcpl. Corner, and Mcpl. Johnson. This was a perfect example of iron sharpening iron. This was the final day of the exercise, the enemy forces had machine gun bunkers on top of the hill, to achieve success we had to take the hill.

Our attack started smoothly we were now 75% up the Hill and suddenly lightning flashes. The skies cracked opened and showers just poured, our footing became difficult, some of us were sliding back down the Hill. We pushed and pushed, a lot of teamwork fire and movement, throwing grenades into the enemy position. At the end we took the Hill, and soon thereafter 'Index' was called (the exercised came to an end). This final attack reminded me of the movie 'Hamburger Hill'. Some of the soldiers walked, others were trucked back and others were driven back in their section Anti-Personnel Carriers (APC).

It was now early May and the freedom of the cities of Fredericton, Moncton and Quebec City were to be celebrated. I was a member of the honour Guard which travelled to those cities. I was fortunate to have as my Guard Commander, Company Sargent Major (CSM) Jimmy Frazier. The reason I am making this statement, while living in Toronto, many have said to me that for people of colour "to win or be successful in life you have to work three times as hard," and some of them continue to make that statement.

I don't believe that. Not for a minute. It is my firm belief that all you have to do is get up and work, work hard to win. It's not about Black, White, Red, Brown or Yellow. It is just about the work. I witnessed in Gagetown that summer three Black Company Sergeant Majors (CSMs) plying their trade to the highest level and they were God-like and free. They had encountered everything the infantry offered, and when they walked on a parade square you could literally hear a pin drop.

After six weeks of training it was time to showcase a masterpiece in precision drill. Imagine 400 infantry soldiers in scarlet uniforms marching through the City of Fredericton to pipes and drums. We were all like Peacocks with our chests out, stomachs in and putting our swag on.

I felt the pride bursting out of my scarlet jacket while executing those precision drill movements on the march, We were the best of the best, full of confidence, energy, and good looks. We were young, and we were ready to stand on Guard for Canada.

Shortly thereafter, a number of us received our posting messages to West Germany. We were given a short leave to visit family and friends, and then it was off to serve the nation.

Chapter 2: The Cold War

The Cold war was rooted in the collapse of the British-American-Soviet Alliance. The Soviets placed and kept local communist parties in power as puppet Governments in once independent countries across Eastern Europe, without due process. The creation of the 'Iron Curtain' according to Prime Minister Winston Churchill in 1946 stated that: "An Iron Curtain had descended across the European Continent."

The Cold War occurred because of actions taken by the Soviet Union and President Truman's introduction of containment of the Soviet Union through the Truman Doctrine. The "Cold War" quite clearly was planned out strategically by the Victors of the Second World War, they would share the spoils, divide the World, distribute and bombard propaganda (obscuring and repackaging the truth) messages to have the masses living in fear. The Cold War had a very unique development in history. Without hostile military engagement, it "froze" international relations between countries into ideological paradigms whose boundaries were clearly defined as a struggle between Capitalism and Communism. In fact, post-war Europe went through a period of relative stability. There are some who would argue that the Cold War created a distinct "East-West" hegemony which allowed the USSR to influence several countries in Eastern Europe, and the U.S. led the allied countries in the West.

In many ways, the Cold war created a warm peace throughout the world. The USSR held Eastern Europe together, while the Western nation states continued to develop the countries under their influence. Simultaneously, the Cold War period provided the super powers to fortify their empires, by doing unfair trade with the smaller Eastern European Nations, South, Central and East Asian Countries, African continent, South Central America, and the

Caribbean. Although a few countries entertained communist ideologies, they never really executed it, except for Cuba, which was, and still is, the first communist state in the Caribbean/Americas. Western nations attempted to discipline Cuba, by diminishing relations with them. However, the Canadian government continued to support Cuba through tourism, by sending on average a million Canadians to Cuba per year, in order to boost tourism and the economy. The excellent Prime Minister, Pierre Elliot Trudeau, made that possible.

There is much debate as well as much to debate surrounding the Cold War with respect to definition, dates, motives, effects and outcomes. Key to the future of the debate surrounding the Cold War is it's writing into history, which will serve as a record for informing the future. According to the United States Department of Defense the Cold War is defined as, "a global competition between two ideologies, the Free World, led by the United States, and the Communist World led by the Soviet Union" (Siracusa, 2008:149).

According to this same documentation the duration of the Cold War is said to be lasting from September 2nd 1945 to December 26th 1991, which Joseph M. Siracusa (2008), points out as a time period marking the last day of World War II to the date the flag of the Soviet Union was lowered as per recognition of the United States Congress. However, in actuality the flag of the Soviet Union was lowered for the last time on December 21st 1991. Siracusa hypothesizes that Congress did not want to, "assign the anniversary of the death of communism to the same say as the birth of Christ" (Ibid:149). Later such attempts to rewrite history can be noted in the now debunked 2003 George W. Bush "Mission Accomplished" speech. In a sense the media plays a gatekeeper role the writing of history and thus the memory of events.

At first glance the Cold War may seem irrelevant today and an ever expanding "fading" memory as Siracusa suggests given that: "Today's high school students were merely infants when the infamous Berlin Wall fell in 1989" (Ibid). However, a closer look reveals it's inscribe into today's society. This notion of a "fading" memory is rebutted by Whitaker and Hewitt, with respect to "Cold War thinking" and not only its relevance but existence today, which they explain via the United States response to the events of September 11, 2001.

It was a time of fear (Ibid,) laying the foundations for today's fear mentality informing international politics "Who is to blame...and which side contributed most to the way in which the Cold War developed?" (Ibid: 151) This is common to the popular types of answers sought and literature written attempting to give clarity to the Cold War period in history, all of which is very much dependent on the time, philosophical position and from what region of the world the commentary is coming from.

Looking to another source in the hopes of defining what the Cold War was and what it means in today's world. A common theme arises: paradigms of opposition—Manichaeism, often essentialist in nature, wrapped in orientalism. According to Whitaker and Hewitt the war was, "an ideological and cultural clash between capitalism and communism, imperialism and socialism, freedom and totalitarianism, democracy and dictatorship, godliness and atheism, and so on" (Whitaker and Hewitt, 2002:6).

Another source highlighting Canada's relationship and involvement in the Cold War situates the War as lasting, "for more than four decades, from the latter half of the 1940s to the end of the 1980s" (Ibid: 5).

The Cold War effects go beyond the mere dissolution of the war, regardless of which dates are adopted, having effectively established what Whitaker and Hewitt have referred to as "Cold War thinking." "Its effects on Canadian society and politics were far ranging and long lasting" (Ibid). This mindset or assumptions the war instilled within society has, "shaped successive generations of Canadians, both in support and in conviction" (Ibid: 6). Playing into divisionary paradigms, the us versus them or good verse evil mindset, a tactic whereby the identified enemy is dehumanized, authorizing the use of force (Robben, 2010:13). This ideological or cultural Cold War thinking would serve as the foundation for future endorsement of Canadian involvement in international relations involving violence and suffering. This can be noted in the Canadian military international involvement in Iraq, Afghanistan, Libya, Bosnia and Somalia, in the years following the Cold War, which did not necessarily take into account the political histories or ethnic-religious complexities of these regions (Ibid: vii).

When assessing Canada's role in the Cold War, issues arise in locating literary accounts and works on the topic. While there is much literature available with respect to for example the United States involvement in the war, literature documenting Canada's participation is limited. In terms of military participation Canada played a limited role, taking part in only one Cold War battle in Korea from 1950 to 1953 (Ibid:5-6).

While the Cold War was largely an American crusade, which explains the abundance of works on the United States and the Cold War, the lack of sources on Canada speaks to a legacy and history of softening the association of Canada in violence and suffering. Whitaker and Hewitt (2002) explain the Cold war period as important in shaping, "Canada's perception of their place in the world," with respect to its role in and contributions to international peacekeeping (Whitaker and Hewitt, 2002:58). Whitaker and Hewitt make it clear that although themes such as peacekeeping, internationalism and Cold War solidarity with its allies was important to Canada's international policy promotion, national interest such as economic interests were central and played a decisive role in domestic politics also important consideration in evaluating successive Canadian international intervention(Ibid:59).

While Canada's combat role in the Cold War can be understood as limited, its role in decades long, two-sided, ideological-political struggle marked by years of international aggression, should not be overlooked. As early as the 1940s, following the Second World War Canada became an original signatory to the North Atlantic Treaty Agreement (NATO) pledging military against the Soviet Bloc and the Warsaw Pact (Whitaker and Hewitt, 2002, p.13). While it may have not been until August 1950 that Canada first engaged into the Cold War militarily sending ground troops, of which included the Princess Patricia's infantry which would some fifty years later serve in Afghanistan, in the UN military intervention in Korea, Canada participated throughout in the form of international relations, breaking from Britain as a new international actor in the global sphere (Whitaker and Hewitt, 2002:69-70). For example, in the 1950s Canada along with the United States formed the North American Aerospace Defense Command (NORAD) (Whitaker and Hewitt, 2002, p.65). In 1957 the two countries established (NORAD) North American Air Defense Command, to provide joint control over continental Air Defense. Furthermore, the Canadian Government allowed the US to access Canadian bases especially Labrador. That space was granted as a staging area for potential bombing runs against Soviets. It also allowed them to fly Bombers over Canada. Lastly, the US built and manned (DEW) Distant Early Warning System (line stations), radar installations that tracked air activity in Canada's Artic.

Canada's participation in the Cold War as a NATO member seemed to emulate the United States, with respect to foreign policy and social trends. Canada did have its own distinct experience of the Cold War (Sendsikas and Cavell, 2005:1162). Just as Whitaker and Hewitt (2002) speak to the unique manifestation of "Cold War thinking" which developed in Canada during the Cold War, according to Cavell (2004), "Canada fought its own uniquely Canadian Cold War, and thus the Canadian experience must be read differently (Sendsikas and Cavell, 2005:1162)." In keeping with Canada's international integration in the global political sphere and peacekeeping, it was during the Cold War that the ground work was laid for Canada's post-Cold War movement from crisis diplomacy to "strategic concepts emphasizing deterrence" (Ibid;), of the post-Cold War era.

The Cold War period had a profound impact on Canadian society and thinking additionally it also set the tone for Canada's role in relations with Latin America and the Caribbean. The effects and outcomes of which would come full circle, starting in the 1970s, following the revision of discriminatory, immigration policies, in Canada, with the introduction of the Points System and immigrant geographies from this region into Canada and Canadian society. Canadian American defense co-operation reflected the protection of democracy in our region to prevent the USSR from infiltrating with their communist ideology.

The spread and influence of the Soviet Union would come into the Americas backyards, increasing levels of Cold War fear, in the 1950s, with the rise of communist politics and leaders in the Western hemisphere, first with British Guiana and then Guatemala in 1954. The, "perceived threats of communist subversion," coming from South and Central America nations would result in action by both the United States and Great Britain (Soderlund and Briggs, 2001:3). As a result of NATO nations' intervention in British Guiana and Guatemala for their perceived threat to the free world via communist subversion, both countries were, "placed on paths towards long-term dictatorship and political repression (Ibid). Simultaneously, in the Caribbean, Cuba created the biggest threat to America, when Fidel Castro and Che Guevara overthrew Batista regime that was supported by the American government.

A considerable bulk of work on the Cold War was written during the war itself, as "until the early 1990s with little or no expectation that it could or would end soon" (Siracusa, 2001:150). Work that would follow, written in the post-Cold War era, was done so within a context of the War's dissolution and erosion of the everyday fear for which the whole world was living under that at any given moment nuclear warfare could breakout. The Cold War affected the whole world, entering the homes via radio, television, and print media. No matter where one was the events taking place around the world became ingrained in the mindset of those living the Cold War reality, via the media. In this situation the media played a decisive role in informing societies of the Cold War reality—what and how the median portrayed and reported and covered. According to Soderlund and Briggs (2001), "Analysis of press coverage of the 1953 British Guiana and 1954 Guatemala crisis points rather clearly to greater extent that The New York Times framed these events in terms of "communist penetration" of the Western Hemisphere (Soderlund and Briggs, 2001:16). In this sense the media at the time was shaping the reality of fear and contributing to the level of "Cold War thinking" and consciousness.

However, the "Cold War thinking" which Whitaker and Hewitt (2002) have spoken to, the constant mindset of fear of outside invasion and elements, has once again become relevant in the post-9/11 world, speaking to the relevance of the Cold War in contemporary times. The connection between the relevance of the Cold War in the post-9/11 world is something which has been echoed in many present-day works on the Cold War. For example, Sendzikas and Cavell claim,

> *"Any commentary on the excess of the Cold War period appearing today naturally invites comparison to post-9/11 society"* (Sendzikas and Cavell, 2005:1162). *Similarly, according to Whitaker and Hewitt (2002) in speaking on the topic of Canada and the Cold War, "history has a way of suddenly biting back, just when you thing it has relaxed its grip. On September 11, 2001, a dozen years after the fall of the Berlin Wall...suddenly, at the dawn of the millennium, the world was seeing a surrealistic re-run of an old movie of the late 1940s"*

(Whitaker and Hewitt, 2002:6).

A closer look into the effects of the Cold War in societies around the world, particularly in NATO countries reveals its continued relevance, in terms of political economic interests authorised by politics of fear. Immediately following the Cold War, a shift in NATO focus occurs from the former USSR to the Islamic world, with the creation of a new enemy—the Near East, latent in Orientalism and national interest. Canadian international intervention to follow long before the so-called war on terror has been according to Sean M. Maloney (2002) convoluted by "the creation of a national peacekeeping myth," pushed by policymakers and its role in Canadian national security policy (Maloney, 2002: xi). "The similarities between the 1950s war against the 'red menace' and the current 'war on terror'," is something that has been noted in recent literature speaking to the Cold War (Sendsikas and Cavell, 2005:1162). The break between the wait of the Cold War in the period directly following the war up until the post-9/11 war on terror, is a misguided discontinuity that obscures and diminishes international intervention which occurred during this period. Maloney

(2002) suggests that the existence of a national peacekeeping myth in Canada and its acceptance by Canadians has, "sometimes drove Canada to commit to dubious peacekeeping operations throughout the 1990s," including those in Somalia (1993), Rwanda (1994), Zaire (1996), and the Persian Gulf War of 1990-91 (Maloney, 2002: xi).

According, to Maloney, this myth is a result of the confusion between ideals and historical reality (Maloney, 2002:2). Looking at the Canadian role in the Cold War, the beginnings of this confusion can be noted with respect to ideals. In setting itself apart from Britain and creating space for itself in the international political area it is during the early years of the Cold War that Canada began to promote itself as a peacekeeper (Whitaker and Hewitt, 2002:59).

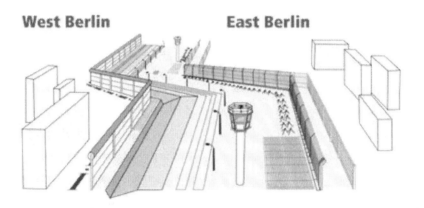

NATO is a western security pact designed to defend Western Europe against soviet invasion, which Canada was a member. The above German wall was constructed to ensure that the West Germans will not cross over into the Eastern side. The space in between the walls is where the East German citizens will be shot-down in an attempt to achieve freedom. The soldiers in the towers were on watch twenty fours, every day and night, until the Wall came down in 1989.

Canada was part of the mission that fought communist North Korea and Chinese forces supported by Soviets, between the years 1950-53. Canadian armed forces and political leaders took action against communist in Latin America, Middle East and Asia. Simultaneously continued to prepare for possible war in Europe.

Canada's commitment to NATO on the continent consisted of an Army Brigade group in West Germany and an Air Force with fighter jets capable of carrying Nuclear weapons. For both the Canadian

Government and its' citizens, the fear of Nuclear War between the US and the Soviet Union remained ever present through the 1950's, 1960's, 1970's and 1980's until November 1989.

On June 17th 1983 I was now in West Germany as a member of 3RCR infantry battalion who was part of 2CMBG (Canadian Mechanized Brigade), which was, part of NATO command, part of the multinational forces Western Europe.

> *"The negative image we have of German people is clearly the result of propaganda. As a Canadian soldier, with a medium tan, I was welcomed by all the German people I made contact with. I played soccer/football with two German teams in the four years that I was stationed in Germany. German people were and still are a hardworking and strong people. They believe in community and it was the first country where I saw women as very independent and empowered. Germans are resilient people. One must always remember that within every ethnic group, every nation state, there exists a group of good people and a smaller group with negative and even evil qualities. There exists the good people who are hard-working and constructive, who focus and spend all their energy on building their nation. And there is also the evil few whose actions are destructive to any sense of progress and nationhood. Although the Western media often blames all German people for the crimes that occurred during World War II, any sound mind that has come to know German people understands that the Nazis were an aberration, a deviation, from the hopeful, cooperative and industrious spirit of German people. German society is a model society, even though a few evils, such as the skinheads and neo-Nazis, may still persist in its margins."*
> - Salick

"Salick, you used to run like the wind." Allan Edison; 2014

A few months from now will be the 2CMBG track and field events taking place in Lahr West Germany. I was selected to be a member of the 400 meters Team of six to be specific. Then, while training our team trainer/Coach/manager (Sgt. Harrington) approached and stated he liked my technique and training towards the event hence he questioned my knowledge. I explained to him I had an opportunity to train with one of Canada's best 400 meter runners, Carson Petrie for one year. I ran the event in 49 seconds flat at LOSSA and right after I received an injury which kept me out of any further competition that year. He then asked me to coach and train, while he manages the team for the upcoming games. I was in disbelief to have been given this responsibility, however I embraced the opportunity and commenced coaching and training the team. The boys were very appreciative of my knowledge and ability therefore we worked as an explosive team. Simultaneously I played soccer/football and European Handball for my Company team, soccer for the Battalion team, CFB Baden team and Hugelsheim F.C. At this moment I was living a dream that I never dreamt.

A couple of days before the games while playing soccer for the base team I sprained my right ankle, the regular drill; Rest, Ice, Compression, Elevation, along with a few Motrin pills to get rid of the inflammation and swelling. I was given a couple extra strong painkillers, if I decide to run. One of the boys got injured (pulling a muscle) while attempting to qualify for the 400 metres final. I saw the medic and I had no other choice but to run. I was given a tensor bandage more like a sock with the painkillers, I was very good, to go.

The race began nearing the end of the day; we completed the event with a third place finish in the final. The games came to an end and we were now ready for the biggest NATO exercise in Europe. (Fall Ex) this is what we do. Could you imagine five nations America, Canada, France, West Germany and the Great Britain. Soldiers all training together coordinating infantry and tank tactics to prepare for the enemy who is literally behind the wall. This exercise went on for two months. Here I am running alongside a German tank firing my C2 at targets ahead of me and the German tank engaging enemy targets to keep their heads down while we advance, now that is powerful. Fall Ex came to an end, some of us were selected for different infantry QL3 courses.

While the majority continue to prepare for war, we had to be combat ready at all times, this my friends is the infantry. After our winter training exercise, we were once again selected for more courses. I was selected to train with the French commando course team to represent our unit and our Country (I was humbled and honoured to represent the Canadian Infantry in this competition). The five nations were as follows; Canada, America, France, West Germany and Great Britain. This was an infantry competition designed by the French Foreign legion. It was an opportunity to demonstrate our infantry skills, fitness level by conquering obstacles that were placed before us, and most of all a lot of teamwork. For example, on average we had two hours sleep, within every twenty four hours over three weeks. Our leaders were in a different state of consciousness, they were infantrymen to the highest level, I will always remember them Sgt. John Cochrane and Mcpl. Vic Hickey. Their birthright was that of the infantry and much more.

The competition started with a force march, complete battle order and 40 Pound pack on your back. We left the start point in 10 minute intervals, the Americans were ahead of us, our mission was basically to pass them on the run. It was fierce, they felt us on their heels, that morning it was ordained by God that we will leave the Americans in the dust. As we passed them we felt that they would be our competition. We then saw the Germans ahead they had a couple injuries, which slowed them down (in the Infantry your team is as fast as the slowest member), in the end we passed them. Throughout the competition the wits and skills of our leaders and our physical state, along with our never say die attitude could not be compared with any of the teams on the competition. We won the competition with the fastest times in the areas where points were awarded; we were now the best infantry platoon among NATO Forces Western Europe. I remember receiving my French commando badge at the awards Ceremony Breisach, France. I looked to my left sleeve the Canadian flag appeared brighter than most days, I brought my left sleeve up and I kissed the flag saying to myself, 'Thank You Canada'. I knew that my fellow soldiers/demigods around me might not understand, as a new Canadian, with a strong accent they embraced me throughout the competition, because as a team we all gave a 100% and then some. Canada gave me a new life, one of hope and dreams and to make it, really all I had to do was work hard and respect people, and for me, that is the simplest solution to success.

Canadians were active at various levels in trying to avoid such a calamity. "We lived every day as though it was our last" (Salick). I was posted to West Germany once again in July 1983 as a member of NATO (North American Treaty Organization) forces Europe, we trained as an International force to oppose communism. We trained hard and fast, we were infantry soldiers, the majority of us lived life for today. The reason for this approach was simple, it was a time of (NBCW) Nuclear Biological Chemical Warfare and we knew as soldiers it would be difficult to survive a nuclear blast. We would train in gas suits with masks, running, shooting, drinking water and eating rations. In the early hours in the morning the siren would sing aloud on the North Marg and where ever the soldiers were, they would report in for duty. We will be deployed immediately into our areas of responsibility along the East – West border/wall.

It was a harsh reality to acknowledge I would have to fight and kill those soldiers on the other side of the wall or those sitting with their machine guns on top of the wall who were ready to engage us because of the differences in political ideologies. During the cold war we were trained to kill the "commie bastard," not fully understanding the political ideologies that divided the world, which created a cold peace between the Eastern and Western Bloc.

We were boys willing to give our Lives in service to Canada, these Boys are my heroes, and would always be my Heroes, as I remember some of them: Dean Salick, my brother, we will play basketball together and what talent he had, naturally gifted, Dave Kearly, Rick Keizer, Dean Turner, Pat Greene, Alan Edison, Lloyd Button, Frank Keats, Tony Lambert who will train me in the art of kick boxing. Sgt. Morrissey my Platoon warrant who was one of my role models, he represented the Sgt. Rock, the American character of a hard leader, however he was Canadian. Paul Soulliere as we will go boxing in the gym and he was also part of the weapons detachment team of our Platoon. We represented the fire- power in the section, there was Kelly Smith(RIP) and Paul Mason as we played soccer for the unit and base team together.

I remember playing tackle football with the boys without equipment on Sundays at 1300 hours whenever we were on the base. The likes of Al King and Dave Shirley, two hard core individuals, body fat did not exist on those two characters, unbelievable, they were seasoned soldiers. I was so young and there were other boys younger than me. We were from different parts of Canada, some of us with different cultural background pursuing one mission, safeguarding the ideology of Democracy, 'the free world' opposing the ideology of communism. We trained as an International force (NATO Forces). We trained hard, we measured our body fat to see how lean we were, now that is fitness (hence the term, lean, green, mean, fighting machine and we represented that slogan). We focused heavily on tank and infantry combined warfare and Nuclear Biological Chemical Warfare (NBCW). U.S. and Canada relations at home to defend our borders against Soviet infiltration.

An ordinary day in West Germany looked like the following: Up at 0530 in the morning, shave, shower and get ready for Physical Training (PT), form up for roll call, go on a 20 kilometer run, after the run, do some Pugil Stick fighting (the king of that training was Sgt. Laidlaw, one fierce individual).

We would then run back to the shacks, shower and change into our combats and go to the mess hall for breakfast and back to the roll call area (North Marg) for more training. The first part of the training would be weapons handling, stripping and assembling the C-7, C-9, C-6 and the 9mm. Beretta, blindfolded. There would be a round robin competition at the end. I will always remember Alex Hogan (RIP), saying "Slick the boy from the Rock(Newfoundland) is too fast for you," and he will smile as always, I would be half-a second or second behind. That Bryan Saulnier and Daniel Ruest were naturally born for the infantry was demonstrated through professionalism and their ability. Thereafter we would entertain some Nuclear Biological Chemical Warfare Training; a gas mask in nine seconds will save your life. Then, we will dress in the complete suit and run in between the anti-personnel carriers as they move forward, also we will execute mine clearance training in an area where mines will be placed. We will then go for lunch to the mess hall, some of the boys will go to Sally-Ann's a snack bar on the base, because most of the base had lunch at the same time.

After lunch we would carry on with AFV recognition of armour vehicle, aircrafts and weapons, right after this we would attend First Aid Classes until 1500 hours. The final 90 minutes we would go in the back 40 and brush up on our "Pepper Pot" skills, the count up 2-3 down, simultaneously in a zig-zag approach to the enemy position. We were always aware that the enemy have a split second before they hit us. After 120 minutes our day of training ended. We would race to the mess hall, have a snack, work on our personnel strength and development training. Personally the day finishes around 1800 hours and thereafter I would travel to Hugelsheim where I would train with the local football/soccer team.

I would get back to the shacks at 2030 hours and now I will prepare for the night's activities. "Boys where are we going tonight', I would ask aloud. According to the evening, we had clubs picked out and sometimes we like changing it around a bit. Sometimes we would be at a club and the DJ stops the music and he will state "all NATO troops stand to, stand to, which means we to get back to our bases and prepare for war. All forces have an area of the wall which we would defend. "This is the Life, no rest for the wicked, ha, ha." We would get back from the club on average, 0430 hours and we would get ready for the next days' training. The saying goes "If you are willing to hoot with the Owls in the wee hours of the morning, you better be ready to scream with the Eagles in the day'". "While on this Earth, we will live hard and fast, we will not waste the moment."

CYPRUS

Cyprus the island of Venus, the birthplace of Aphrodite, it's a beautiful, tranquil island at the crossroads of past and present great civilizations in the middle of the Mediterranean, between Syria, Egypt, Turkey and Greece. Cyprus has a rich history that reaches back to the Paleolithic period. Taking form and force during the Bronze Age, with the beginning of cities and the copper trading/mining. Cyprus means copper and from the 15th century BC., it had already claimed that name. On this small island with 9000 years of civilization, culture and history, the dominant population 80% are Greek Cypriots that trace their linkage to Greek culture and history since 1800BC and the 18% Turks trace their history to the Ottoman Empire since 1500 AD.

The geographic setting of the island has been both a blessing and a curse; it has a long and deep history of invasions and been conquered by every powerful and some minor historical groups in the Middle East. The conquerors have had a strong influence on the physical, natural and cultural environments of the island. Consequently, because of its maritime roads and strategic outpost for the core empire, Cyprus was of interest to ruling armies from the Assyrians, Persians, Egyptians, Romans, Venetians, Turks and English (just to mention a few).

Ottoman rule in Cyprus began in 1571 and for the first time a Moslem community was established in the island. Privileges were given to the Orthodox church of Cyprus, from the beginning of Ottoman rule, giving it not just religious authority but also political authority. Cyprus went through hard times during Ottoman rule. The contribution of the Greek Cypriots to the Greek War of Independence in 1821 resulted in the execution of Cyprus Archbishop Kyprianos, three of his bishops and about 470 clerics and laymen.

The modern Cyprus question begins in 1878 Britain in a secret agreement with the Ottoman government took over Cyprus, first as a protectorate and then annexed the island on the "outbreak of war with the Ottoman Empire in 1914, which became a Crown Colony in 1925." One of the reasons for occupying Cyprus was to protect the Ottoman Sultan against Russia, but it's more obvious, the unmentioned role, was defense of the Suez Canal, in which Britain had acquired an interest

Cypriots had early expectations of substantial changes in their political, economic and social lives. They desired the union of Cyprus and Greece to be fulfilled, however, this would not materialize. Greek Cypriot disappointment with British colonial rule together with the prevailing economic recession, led to the uprising events of October 1931. In the Greek-Cypriot community the demand for "enosis" (unity) developed rapidly from the 1930s, the turning point being the Greek-Cypriot riots of 1931 and the burning down of Government House. These events resulted in even harsher colonial measures being imposed by the British. The Greeks of Cyprus continued to press on with their demand for national restitution and union with Greece however the British government continued to reject it. On 15th January 1950 a referendum on union with Greece was held, in which 95. 7% of Greek Cypriots voted in favour. The referendum outcome had no effect on the British stance. On 20th October 1950 Bishop of Kition Makarios III was elected as Archbishop. The political deadlock that the Greek Cypriots faced led to the waging of the national liberation anti-colonial struggle of 1955-59, by the National Organisation of Cypriot Fighters (EOKA). The struggle resulted in the ending of British rule, but not to union with Greece. The Zurich-London Agreements led to the establishment of the independent Republic of Cyprus. On 13th December 1959 Archbishop Makarios III was elected first President of the Republic and Dr. Fazil Kutchuk first Vice President.

We must not forget that as a consequence of the British handling of the situation, Turkey was reintroduced to the picture as an interested party in Cyprus in the 1950s, a fact which had a negative effect on the evolution of events afterwards.

Greek Cypriots who make up the vast majority of the people of Cyprus was at that time "enosis" or union with Greece. For the Turkish Cypriot community, the goal was taksim or partition. Cypriot independence was achieved through many years of struggle, with several compromises of the policies of the colonial power. That in pursuit of its own interests refused to grant Cypriots the inalienable right of self-determination. In most colonies, this is what happens, struggles and compromising of colonies.

At the same time, the policies of enosis (union with Greece) and of taksim (partition) exacerbated problems in the functioning of the state which was in itself difficult anyway. Cooperation and confidence between the communities suffered even more and the chasm between the communities widened with the result of the inter-communal clashes of 1963 and 1967, the withdrawal of Turkish Cypriots and the creation of enclaves in which the Turkish Cypriots were isolated.

The first act of the play of partition was played with the inter-communal clashes and the second with the fascist coup of the Greek junta and EOKA-B (Greek-Cypriot paramilitary organization), and the Turkish invasion in the summer of 1974, which led to the occupation of 37% of Cyprus' territory. Since then Cyprus and its people have remained de facto divided.

According to Glen Camp (2001), the cold war unrealistic fear of the Russian "Evil Empire" and the U.S. "obsession with the Soviet Union was responsible for a good deal of the Cyprus tragedy" (Camp, 2001:1). The irony is that both the obsession and the tragedy were unnecessary from either a geopolitical or moral point of view. The Soviet threat could have been contained by largely economic and more nuanced military means at far less cost to all involved, including Cyprus.

> *"Cyprus was, nevertheless, a 'non-aligned' state much to the impotent fury of Washington. Indeed, Makarios was often referred to as 'he Castro of the Mediterranean' even though he allowed American U-2 spy-planes to fly from British bases in Cyprus and permitted vital British and US electronic monitoring stations to operate throughout the island. Moreover, the Cypriot communist party, Akel, upon which he depended for maintaining his position, was Euro-communist and relatively independent of Moscow. But to many US leaders, all communist parties were alike, just as all communists were alike. A nuanced understanding of the Soviet threat was absent. Rational diplomats, such as George Kennan, the originator of 'containment', complained that Washington over militarised the Cold War. But to John Foster Dulles, America's 'misguided missile' as Adlai Stevenson termed him, the Cold War was a Manichaean struggle. One wonders at the subconscious motivations of both superpowers which explain this mirror image, each seeing the other as an evil, aggressive adversary. Without it, the Cyprus tragedy might have been avoided, as might the Vietnam and Soviet–Afghan wars, for in foreign policy, perception is often more important than reality since 'nothing is but thinking makes it so'* (Camp, 2001:3).

Sigmund Freud observes, in 'civilization and Its Discontents,' that "it is precisely communities with adjoining territories, and related to each other in other ways as well, who are engaged in constant feuds and in ridiculing each other." He titles this phenomenon as 'the narcissism of minor differences.' Psychiatrist, Vamik Volkan (1979), parallels this observation in his book, Cyprus – War and Adaptation, when he attaches the phenomenon to groups like the English and Irish, Arabs and Jews, and finally the Turks and Greek, "especially on the island of Cyprus where the proximity has been so close." Freud's book was published in 1930, and Volkan's in 1979, it seems as though even now in the 21st century, humanity hasn't learned how to put aside these minor differences, in the name of peace. Volkan grasps that individuals derive their identity with a nation, its people, its customs and above all, with land defined by definite borders. The Greeks and Turks so strongly identify with the land as their own, since "boundaries… come to be related to the continuity and dimensions of the self," this is the reason there is so much conflict and the purpose for the green line within the island (Volkan). Cyprus' history is one of a great nation. In August of 1960, Cyprus became the Republic of Cyprus, and in 1963, the Greeks attacked the Turks, inciting the creation of the green line. Volkan continues to discuss that "a people who define themselves as comprising a nation…but who cannot give it geographic actuality, live in constant condition of injured self-regard and inner rage." The accomplishments of the Cyprus nation cannot be identified as Greek success or Turkish success, that along with the green border separating the nationalities, causes lack of geographic certainty, causing the rage we see exemplified in the conflicts on the island. Volkan quotes an Israeli journalist who wrote about the conflict in Israel, saying "We are not fighting each other. We fight masks of the devil that each side has painted on the other." The conflict between the Greeks and Turks is one of notions fed down through the decades of what one side believes the other is, and not what actually is. For example, Greek Cypriots nationalist teachings are believed to be directly successful, however the work of education is what evokes a Greek spirit, which is already present in a child. In 'Divided Cyprus', Rebecca Bryant writes an article, "On the condition of post-colonialist in Cyprus," where she quotes a eulogy addressed to the first contingent of Boy Scouts. The speech conveys an idea of "immaterial power" that is the history of the race. This then evokes "orgasmic thrill" and "an organic shudder" that leaves them "spiritually prostate" before the glory of the Greek flag. (Bryant, 54, 55). George Orwell, writes that "the nationalist not only does not disapprove of atrocities committed by his own side, but he has remarkable capacity of not even hearing about them (Papadakis, 66)."

"On December 21,1964, violence interrupted in Nicosia. Two Turks were killed and five wounded. Turks called this outbreak and the events that followed "the bloody Christmas massacre." (Papadakis,6) The psychological process of Cypriot Turks on which I focus in this book manifested themselves strikingly from 1963 until 1978, three years after the intervention of the Turkish army which divided the island into two sectors, the northern one becoming Turkish and the southern Greek.

Greek and Turkish writers naturally disagree over the cause of the crisis and Christmas time in 1963, which signaled the beginning of a series of bloody events. American observers (Keefe et al., 1971) asserted, "it was neither a carefully planned Turkish rebellion, as the Greeks maintained, nor a systematic attempt to exterminate the Turkish population, as some of the Turkish spokesmen alleged." Nevertheless, the average Turk did feel that this was the beginning of extermination, and I suspect that the average Greek felt that the Turks had started systematic rebellion.

By December 23, 1963, Nicosia, the capital of Cyprus, had become a battleground. Each side took hostages and brought charges of atrocity against each other. Since it was physically impossible for Turkish Cypriot minister and members of the House of Representatives to attend meetings of the Parliament, which met in the Greek sector, they were effectively excluded. None wanted to risk their lives to attend, whatever their views. Thus control of the legal government of the Republic of Cyprus fell in to the hands of Cypriot Greeks only, which was considered unlawful by the Turks. Since that time there has been no cooperation of any kind in government and the polarization of the two groups has become increasingly fixed.

Canada played a significant role in Cyprus during its constitutional crisis of 1963-1964. Canada's largest peacekeeping mission began a few years after the Suez crisis in 1959. In 1963 antagonisms between the two communities threatened to bring into armed conflict and intervention the mother countries Turkey and Greece. From the beginning:

> "[A]s a member of both NATO and the British Commonwealth, of which Cyprus also held membership, Canada understood the consequences of instability within its international groupings. Though both organizations tried to assemble a peacekeeping force between January and March, the Cypriots continually vetoed the proposals in favour of the United Nations"

(Journal of Military and Strategic Studies).

The failed diplomatic efforts to resolve the crisis of the UN Security Council forced the "Turkish ultimatum of 12 March, 1964 that reawakened efforts to resolve the crisis.

It is important to note that, "Canada's Secretary of State for External Affairs Paul Martin Sr. responded with assertive diplomacy. Martin successfully led a personal telephone campaign to gain assurances that Britain, Canada, Ireland and Sweden would participate in a UN force" (Paul Martin, 1985:457).

"In 1964, Canadian soldiers made up the first international contingent to arrive in Cyprus to defuse a crisis when ethnic violence between the Greek-Cypriot majority and Turkish Cypriot minority threatened to spiral into war in the Mediterranean between Greece and Turkey. For 29 years, Canada joined other countries in contributing contingents to the United Nations Force in Cyprus (UNFICYP). Peacekeepers on the island patrolled the Green Line, a narrow buffer zone between the two combatants, and reported on troop movements and ceasefire violations. In 1993, with the Canadian government facing mounting demands for military support to UN missions in more pressing and dangerous conflicts in Africa, the Former Republic of Yugoslavia, and elsewhere, Canada ended its major commitment to UNFICYP. Today, one Canadian staff officer remains in UNFICYP headquarters to show the flag while soldiers returning from Afghanistan enjoy the island's beaches"

(Andrew Burtch, 2010).

"The Cyprus mission is historically significant for Canada for a number of reasons. Over 20,000 Canadians served there from 1964 to 1993, many on multiple tours. It represents Canada's longest "traditional" peacekeeping mission, where an armed but impartial UN force was invited by both sides in the conflict to keep the peace until a diplomatic solution could be found. Canada's decision to supply troops to the Cyprus mission satisfied our national Interests as defined in Cold War foreign and defence policies. Canadian support for peacekeeping largely served the goals of the Western alliance: a peacekeeping force in Suez in 1956 prevented Soviet military intervention in the Middle East, and the force in Cyprus prevented Greece and Turkey, two NATO partners, from warring over the island, which housed strategic British naval and air bases" (Ibid).

Canada agreed to send forces to Cyprus in March 1964, Arthur Andrew, Canada's High Commissioner to Cyprus, warned his superiors, "Should it be decided to send troops, on present form in my judgment it will not repeat not be a short or easy job" (Ibid). For the first ten years of the mission, Cyprus posed few dangers for Canadian troops, whose tours comprised six monotonous months of duty in fixed observation posts.

In July 1974, however, a Greek-inspired coup overthrew the Cypriot president, Archbishop Makarios III, and installed a former leader of a Greek-Cypriot terrorist cell intent on enosis, political union of Cyprus with Greece. Within days, the Turkish armed forces dusted off their 1964 invasion plans and sent 40,000 troops to assault the island with the stated intention of securing the Turkish minority.

Early in the morning of July 20, 1974, Cypriots awakened to the sound of Turkish aircraft and saw Turkish paratroopers land on the plateau between Nicosia's Turkish sections. The air attacks and the troop landings from the sea near Kyrenia secured a corridor between Nicosia and Kyrenia within three days. The fighting was brutal in the extreme. Subsequent activity of Turkish troops in August secured the northern 37 percent of the island within two days. Markids (1977) estimates Greek losses during the war as 6,000 dead and 3,000 missing and Denktash (1977) estimates Turkish losses as 1,500 dead and 2,000 wounded. As a result of the Turkish military intervention, Sampson gave up the presidency, and the Greek junta fell.

The Turkish military intervention cut the island in two. Turkish Prime Minister Bulent Ecevit declared a cease-fire and announced that "we are now in a situation where the foundations have been laid for the new Federal State of Cyprus." There was an inevitable sequel of social turmoil, and a new series of tragic events. About 160,000 Cypriot Greeks become refugees, fleeing toward the south from the Turks; and about 65,000 Cypriot Turks began a slow trek toward the north. EOKA B fanatics, angered at the failure of the United States to prevent the Turkish intervention, assassinated the American ambassador to Cyprus (Cyprus – War and Adaptation, pg. 24 - 26)

As Andrew Burtch (2010) points out in the statement below:

> *"The United Nations force was caught in the middle of the war. Four hundred and fifty soldiers of 1 Commando, Canadian Airborne Regiment were caught in the capital city of Nicosia Under fire from both sides, UNFICYP repeatedly sought to secure local ceasefires and, when these failed, the Canadian contingent placed strategic assets such as Nicosia International Airport and the Ledra Palace Hotel under UN control as a means of limiting the conflict. Seventeen Canadians were wounded in the fighting, and Privates Gilbert Perron and Jean-Claude Berger were killed by rifle fire. In one incident on 23 June at Camp Kronberg, north of Nicosia, Canadians were forced to return fire at Greek forces that attacked a patrol leading Turkish soldiers back to their lines under UN protection. Lasting only a few minutes, the firefight was the Canadian army's first combat since the Korean War. In reaction to these firefights, the Trudeau government doubled the Canadian presence on Cyprus and provided soldiers with*

armoured personnel. Canadians were forced to return fire at Greek forces that attacked a patrol leading Turkish soldiers back to their lines under UN protection."

On February 15th, 1986 in the service of peace my fellow peacekeepers and I arrived in Cyprus. We were part of operation "SNOWGOOSE" that is Canada's commitment and contribution to the UN force in Cyprus which began in 1964-1993 and cost 27 Canadian personnel their lives. The UNFICYP's mandate was to monitor the cease-fire between Greek and Turkish Cypriots and to patrol a demarcation line (Green line) across the island. My first thoughts and observations correlated with the military and public newspapers of the danger facing the UN-a constant reminder of the uneasy peace and periodic violence -from both Turkish and Greek Cypriots. I was very well aware of the heroic, neutral and brave actions of the Canadian contingent in the 1974 Turkish invasion that protected both communities under great risk and danger. For example, the airport, and Ledra palace incidents and the events at Camp Kronberg. It was determined by the Globe and Mail that at Camp Kronberg Canadians fired and killed for the first time since Korea. Canadians fired on Greek ambushers protecting Turks and their own force.

DEAN SALICK (BROTHER):

From the very beginning, I became aware of the complexity and difficulty of our mission in the maintenance of peace. For example, while preparing for the Canadian contingent show I was the driver for the Lt. Colonel in Nicosia. One day as I was driving him from Ledra Palace hotel to the airport we encountered a large group of Greek protesters outside Ledra Palace chanting and waving banners with the slogan "UN GO Home" and throwing stones at our vehicle. My first thoughts were that the Greeks are irrational and not in full comprehension of the crisis of their situation. How could the Greeks have survived the Turkish invasion of Cyprus without UN intervention and participation, I asked myself? The continuous preparation and monitoring of the cease-fire between Greek and Turkish Cypriots and patrolling the demarcation line (Green line) across Nicosia was our duties. We were trained to expect the unexpected as violent and periodic acts of aggression took place between the two communities. The 'Beaver lodge' incident where after the completion of our foot patrol at the Green Line with Cpl. Smith, we were ordered on high alert due to Turkish activity outside Beaver lodge. A big march, of Turkish Cypriots infront of Beaver lodge were chanting for more land rights for Turks. We were all on "Stand Too/100%," which means that all our soldiers must be on high alert and expect the unexpected, then it changed to 75% so that we have some soldiers rest because a soldier performs best when they are well rested. This was not the case however as this dragged on for five days and nights as we waited for the UN to make a decision. Sometimes, while on night patrols the Turks will fire at us rather aggressively, we had to keep our heads down and observe while waiting for permission to load our magazines to engage the enemy. On one occasion, local Turkish prisoners escaped we searched and apprehended them on the Turkish side before crossing the Greek demarcation line and exaggerating the threat of aggression to themselves and us.

> "Slick you were always running, playing basketball and soccer." Daniel Ruest 2016

> "Slick you were always there for us." Bryan Saulnier 2016

The peacekeeping military's philosophy and especially mine, is not just to protect and maintain peace however to build bridges of friendship within the local populations. I always believed, in building bridges through sports, and in the infantry other than soldiers we are athletes. I was becoming a machine, representing the Canadian contingent in basketball and soccer. My personal training plan to maintain a high level of fitness were as follows; ran 80 kilometers per week, strength training for 1 hour three days a week also the training sessions with the contingent soccer and basketball teams. I believed in giving the best of the best, because with the maple leaf on my team uniform ask me to give a 100 percent and then some. To represent the contingent team was about my unit and country, it was never about me, I had opportunities to play against military International Teams, Sweden, Denmark, British, and Cyprus airways. I was now living a life that will make the world people jealous. To think in 1977, I was playing basketball and soccer on gravel and pitched schoolyard, with a group of young men who could not afford shoes. I remember, playing soccer, in Trinidad, without footwear because I could not afford it; we loved the game and it kept us away from crime. I find it amazing, that nine years later I have played football in Germany with the Canadian military base team and a Local German team (Hugelsheim F.C.) and now in Cyprus with the UNIFCYP League. (*Just to think about the aforementioned makes my heart race and swell with pride of achievement*).

Football/soccer/sports when organised fairly and properly, has the potential to bring nations to a common understanding for Peace and development. Furthermore, it creates financial freedom for those who meet the standard for professional and semi-professional leagues. Simultaneously, it maintains good health among young people, while dissecting and intersecting race/gender/class and sexual orientation inequalities. The Canadian Base team consisted mainly of soldiers of 3RCR, who were already fit and ready for playing soccer. Soccer with the German team was building bridges of friendship. It was an experience of a lifetime, as will be Cyprus, Bosnia and Macedonia.

When my first tour to West Germany ended in September 1984, our RCR battalion's new home was Kapyong Barracks Winnipeg and it was there, in the fall of 1985, I met one of my heroes. Kevin Grieg. He was an exceptional young man and a football/soccer icon with the technical ability, personal skills, and knowledge of the game that was beyond his peers. Our first competitive race was a 1.5-mile race which Kevin won, I placed third that afternoon. Our unit was preparing to go to Cyprus for peacekeeping duty, hence we started a soccer team for the UN league and to play against the locals. The first time I saw the extent of his technical abilities, I automatically assumed this is a national or professional standards. I thought to myself what talent, what discipline, what went wrong?

The national program at the time of question, lacked integrity and hence the selection of players who have the ability to represent Canada were not considered because those in charge focus on their own (because of class ethnic group, and who should have the right to represent Canada). In that period. Kevin would have been a natural selection for that team, life is strange on the positive side, we were fortunate to have him with us. I will admit Kevin inspired me to work harder not only at our training sessions, also even after the session was over we would do extra training to be the best. I could clearly state our team very appreciative of Kevin for his professionalism. We were now on our way to Cyprus to keep peace. CANCON (Canadian Contingent) we represent Canada in the foreign land and were literally ambassadors of Canada.

There are moments playing with Kevin that will linger on in my mind forever. For example, in one battalion game N-coy vs. O –coy from Kevin's boot to my boot, four goals in the opposing net, his touches on the ball and finding the players, his vision remarkable, in the UNFICYP league. Dan Mcmenemy remembers; On August 24th CanCon vs. BritCon (support regiment) although beaten 4 – 3, a free kick from Kevin, he went airborne to complete a bicycle kick, while in the air the wind shifted the ball, from the bicycle kit position his body switched in mid-air, where he was now literally in a lateral position to the ground, pouncing the ball into the net. Many Canadians at the command level thought that with proper preparation we stood a chance of winning the league. We also had the opportunity to play Cyprus Airways one of the local teams.

Photo provided by Wayne Nicholson RIP.

UNFICYP Soccer Tournament

On Tues 8 Apr 86 the UNFICYP Soccer Tournament, the grand finale to the UNFICYP Soccer League, took place at the BBC fields. Each of the teams, having played 20 games over the last 4 months, were eager to display their talent to the Canadians, who had recently traded mukluks for cleats. After losing 3-0 to the Fusiliers and 2-0 to the Scout Car Regt, the CANCON team, with Capt Kok at the helm, surprised the Support Regiment who managed to pull out a last minute 4-3 victory. Qualified observers, surprised at the depth of individual talent noted that if CANCON had more preparation time, the outcome would have been vastly different. The team has an upcoming exhibition game against DANCON, the tournament champs, and against Cyprus Airways — a Div 2 local team.

PRO PATRIA

Pte Derrick Sallick showing a Fusilier how to "break dance", as Sgt Donny Sheppard "moon walks" across the field.

Cpl Kelly Smith (7) getting set to hammer the ball as Cpl Jerry O'Grady and Pte's Kevin Robert "Scotty" Greig look on.

"The way I see it . . ." Capt Kok (5), Cpl Patey, Pte Sallick (8), Pte Cadieux, Capt Buchanan, MCpl Adler, MCpl Sampson, Lt Osborne (sitting) and an unknown member discussing the results of a game.

8 POINT STAR   PAGE 3

3 RCR Basketball Team

On 23 Apr 86 a small but determined team of basketball players from 3RCR ventured down to Ayios Nikolaos (British Base) to play the "Ayi Nic Comm SQD". Although our team was out numbered 13 to 6, we bettered the opposition through team play and conditioning with the final score of 43-37.

3RCR went on the attack right from the initial jump and stayed in the lead for the entire game. The overall offense was nicely masterminded by Lt Mark Osborne making good use of the two big men under the boards via Capt's Mark Gallow and Buck Buchanan.

Excellent hustle and relentless pursuit of the ball was accomplished by MCpl Dave Kearley and Pte "Slick" Salick. A good deal of the scoring went to Pte Dale Booth who handled the outside jump shots and give and goes effectively defeating the opposition's defense.

Overall it was a closely contested match and a hard fought victory for 3RCR. Does this mean another free T-shirt and 2 by 10 miler written off?

"Has anyone seen the ball?"

"Who says you have to dribble the ball!"

It's a bird, a plane...

On August 24, 1986, the Canadian contingent soccer team after playing a fantastic game against the British, few soldiers were given a day pass for August 25th. Here again, as I had stated before, I was living a dream. At 6:30 in the morning, August 25th, my CSM asked me to his office, stated that the game last evening was a fantastic game "you have performed very well in all areas and all tasks while on the Island thus far. When we go back to Canada, I will be sending you on your leadership course." I said, "thank you, sir." He replied, "Enjoy your day off." A few soldiers, my brother, and myself, decided to travel to Ayia Napa resort/beach for rest and relaxation. This was the only opportunity my brother and I had an opportunity to bond since February 15th

We were now driving on the UN road followed by a vehicle with two Danish UN delegates. While driving on the road a Greek Cypriot suicide driver drove his big truck into both our vehicles, killing a Danish doctor and severing the leg of the other Danish passenger The Canadian vehicle which I was in was impacted by the crash and I was thrown 60 meters away from the collision. They found my body in a pool of blood, my bones were sticking out of my body, and my face was smashed, bruised and unrecognizable. The first couple of soldiers that reached the scene thought I was dead. Yet, by the grace of God, two Greek Cypriot nurses arrived a few minutes later, administering first aid stopped the bleeding and told the other soldiers that I was still alive but in a coma. The Greek Cypriot driver was killed on the spot

From August 25th to September 6th, I was in a coma. Left arm broken in three places, piece of bone came out and left out of sight, and I was paralyzed on my left side for the next 6 months. My first tango with death, they say a cat has nine lives, I am wondering how many do I have? The tour ended and I headed back to Canada after a few surgeries and Christmas passed me as a cripple, a useless human being. My left side was paralysis for six months.

New Year's Day 01st, 1987, Kevin came to my door, he could have been out drinking with the boys but came to support me. He said, "bro I cannot see you like this anymore." He took me for my first walk and thereafter walks, walk-run, runs. He literally brought me back from someone who had given up on life, dreaming of yesterday, stuck in the past. He trained and coached me back to a competitive individual running and playing football/soccer again and much more.

Kevin Greig believed in me and gave the kind of support (physically and mentally) to continue my journey in the Infantry. As a matter of fact, I became a stronger and more responsible man, always striving for excellence. A couple months later, the Company Sergeant Major(CSM), called me to his office and asked me, "Cpl. Salick would you like to stay with us or go to another trade? I replied Sir this is my home, my life, my family, what happened sir it was a bump in the road, I will be fit again and I will take on the world sir." He replied calmly, "good that's what I wanted to hear, we will give you the support to help get you to the best physical shape of your life." I replied "thank you sir." In my handicapped state, CSM Hodgson, suggested that I should sign up for university because this injury might be a permanent handicap, acknowledging he was seeking my personal interest.

My unofficial first meeting with Kevin Greig was a bit strange. The reasons for this are as follows; I arrived to Canada on September 11th

1977, in October I joined the Albert Campbell Collegiate cross country junior team, Kevin was also a member of the team. He was younger and ran in his age group his brother was on the team that I ran on. Is it not strange, although we were on the same team we never spoke? At that time the structure in Toronto then focused on division through ethnic make-up and I will argue, today it remains the same. Kevin monitored my health for at least eighteen months.

It was the Grey Cup of 1987, the RCR boys organized their own Grey Cup with the boys from the east coast and the boys from the west coast. Myself with a southern accent was a free agent, I represented the east in the first half and the west in the second half. The game began at 1300 hours, temperature - 30 with strong periodic winds with bright sunshine and 18 inches of snow to trample on. There were no snow plows available to clean the field, ha, ha. The referee approaches the teams, "Grunts" (government rejects unfit for naval training). We have two end zones, a center mark for the field, and a 10-yard chain, rules, play hard, hit hard, and have fun.

My heroes were all around me ready to rough it up. The likes of Tim Duncan, Docherty, Tim and Darryl Barrat, Dave (Horse) Horochuk, Kevin Greig, and myself of course, the one-armed bandit with a fiber glass cast on my left arm recovering with my arm broken in three places.

The game began and the boys were knocking each other out as though large monies were involved. Clothesline everywhere. Bruising, tackling each other, down to the ground. With every play someone was being bruised. After one hour of continuous rough play the game came to an end. It was pure, uncut, it was a massacre. At the games end we all went into the junior ranks. Some were hurting, they had a few drinks to kill their pain. Myself and a few others had to go to the air force base to receive medical attention. In the end result, I had nine toes frost bitten. Others had frost bitten fingers, and just bruises, no broken bones.

Although this was our Grey Cup, I realized that these men were a special breed of human beings, they will give everything on the field, bruise each other, hurt each other, shake hands, huddle, pick each other up from the ground although they play on opposing teams. There was no glory here, there wasn't anything to gain but the pure display of guts and determination to win. I find it so amazing. I have looked at professional Football, the NFL, CFL, rugby, however this Grey Cup game that we played was one of greatest performance by the men of 3RCR. They would put professional players to shame. Hence, this is what my heroes are made of.

For eighteen months I struggled to become healthy, and I was now one of the top distance runners in the unit. For example, the "Great Grain Relay" of Manitoba in the spring of 1988, from 93 teams, Kevin's team won and my team finished third, we were now on our way to West Germany to protect the free world from communism. Kevin also prepared me to level where I was back on the 3rcr Soccer Team.

In 1989 I travelled to Holland with the Canadian Forces Base Baden team to participate in the military junior soccer World. This kind of support and the belief in your brother is rare. To thi s day I always give thanks to Kevin.

We played soccer and participated in running competitions from 1985 to 1986, 88' to 1990, we created a bond as soldiers, as brothers and friends. In 1990, Kevin decided to leave the military temporarily while we were posted to West Germany, to attend York University and upon completion he would re-join the military. In 1991 I was posted to CFB Toronto, as a regular force cadre to a reserve unit. At this moment I would like to say thank you to CSM Joe Bentley and RSM Douglas for accepting my request and giving me the opportunity to commence the pursuit of a University Degree. Kevin completed his degree and was back in the regular force. My process will be longer working full time with the reserves while attending university part time. Constantly awaiting the moment, when my country calls I will go back to my unit for foreign missions. I did not anticipate the struggle to get back in the academic world, considering from 1982 to 1991 I was a soldier only learning about warfare and continuously preparing for nuclear biological warfare and picking up the German language as a personal exercise.

July 12th, 1988, we are now in the foreign land again. Other than our military training, soldiers as myself and Kevin, will sign up and play for local teams. I played for Solingen FC while Kevin, played Rastatt FC, which in many ways allowed us to breakdown social and cultural barriers. For example, in that era many Europeans believed the only game Canadians are good at is Ice Hockey and that was a social construct, which was further developed and bombarded by the media.

In the spring of 1989 the Canadian military team was invited to the military world cup consisting of Western Nations Military Teams. A team was selected and I believed we had six weeks of training, Kevin was the assistant coach/player the head coach was WO. Wright, a peri-staff member, and my name was one of the 24 to train and play in this World Cup. We trained hard for six weeks, as expected a few injuries near the end of final selection, however we had a good team. When we arrived in Holland we were showered with a lot of love, appreciation and respect. I later acknowledged why the Dutch had this respect for us, Canadians soldiers in WWII fought for their freedom and were successful.

The tournament was fantastic, our team made it to the final four, Canada vs. France and England vs. Holland. We were beaten by the French, they played a game of short passes and on occasions they will execute five touches to our goal. This was their game, they played Holland in the final while we played the British for third place, which the British won. It was one of the highlights of my military/soccer career.

I remember these heroes of mine taking me and teaching me the game of ball hockey, mastering it with speed, aggression and a skill set of a defenseman I could not be beaten. It was a game I enjoyed immensely to blow steam away. I loved it.

Imagine a gym or an old ice hockey arena where boys are just smashing and slamming each other into the gymnasium concrete walls or the arena boards with the intent to hurt. It was amazing, maximum aggression, with speed and skills with limited rules; those boys will always be my heroes.

We were now back in Germany getting ready for the local leagues (military and local), We were hoping that activities did not become too hostile, but our task in Germany was coming to an end. In 1990 Kevin decided to take a break from the military and attend York University in Toronto, Canada. In 1990 I requested a posting to Toronto, where I would pursue university education part time.

I literally grew up in the Infantry. I saw boys come and go from a young age, with the intent of giving everything for their country, including their life. What men! I thought to myself.

From the beginning in Cornwallis, Nova Scotia, to Petawawa, Ontario, to CFB Gagetown, and thereafter to Baden, Baden, West Germany, then to Winnipeg Manitoba and then back to West Germany where I witnessed the fall of the Berlin Wall, I felt a strong sense of passionate commitment to the soldier's life. Even so, I embraced the idea of war and peace for development at a young age after viewing the movie "To Hell and Back" with Audie Murphy. Once I had made the decision, I knew that the next step for me would be to pursue a university education. After speaking with my CSM, my wish was granted. However, after receiving my posting message in 1990, the Persian Gulf was just beginning to boil. I didn't hesitate. I attempted to decline my posting so that I could go to the Gulf with my boys 'N Coy.' But I was told that this was not possible, because my posting was less than a month away. I was not happy. I had a silent fear of ending a life that I enjoyed, of losing the family that I had found, and deserting the brotherhood that my boys and I had created. I was part of this rifle company from June 1983 to June 17th 1991. On June 17th 1991, I boarded a plane to Toronto, Canada.

Toronto 1991-1996

The Royal Regiment of Canada
April 27, 1996

Prince Charles (front from center) visit to the Royal Regiment of Canada. Cpl. Salick (Front row, second from left).

THE ROLE OF THE RESERVES

"To Augment the Regular Force and Give Aid to Civil Power."

I arrived on June 17, 1991 to the Royal Regiment of Canada or as some will identify them as the Royal Refugees of Canada. As many intellectuals focus on the history and the ills of Canada, I focus on the present and possibilities of a greater future. At the Regiment, I saw individuals and groups from every cultural make-up that exist in Canada. Intellectuals and journalists who focus on racism and discrimination and attempt to paint Canada as a bad nation, however the present day reality is totally different. I see the aforementioned as excuses for idleness. One must always remember that racism is a social construct that can be deconstructed with the right approach. Simultaneously, we as Canadians must be willing to educate self and others in attempt to deconstruct it.

Here are young men and women who dissected and intersected race, class, sexual orientation and gender. Many ethnic groups comprising of young men and women are given the equal space and job equality to compete physically and mentally to serve Canada. I witnessed first-hand where some young women with their great determination and attitude surpass some of the young men during training. (Attitude- never give up, never quit).

These young men and women enjoy the civilian world where they will attend college or university, in some cases have their own business while training in the reserve units in preparation for war and peace. Hence they are exceptional citizens among their civilian counterparts. Their contribution to Canada is extraordinary, when one considers their dedication, loyalty, and responsibility to Canada. They might not be as well trained as the hardcore regular force soldiers however, their willingness to serve must always be respected. when they call upon for international duty, they give 100%.

I was now part of the Regular Support Staff (RSS) for the Royal Regiment of Canada. I was excited because it gave me an opportunity to take leadership, be more responsible and be an example to future soldiers, those who are willing to give their lives for this blessed country, Canada. At RSS I was given the opportunity to attend York University and pursue a degree in political Science. Many people will ask why politics? Why not physical education because I was very physical. I believe we should develop the brain as I did my body.

There I met an exceptional officer, Captain Walter Perchal 1991, who guided me into the academic world, as a matter of fact he was on the ground to supervise and inspire me, to ensure I obtained my first degree. What was amazing though, at the unit he opened his door to all soldiers. He cared for their development, not only as soldiers however as human beings. He literally dissected the ideologies of race, class, gender, and sexual orientation through accepting all as unique individuals and did his best to prepare them to be successful in life. This exceptional quality was also extended to his university students where I was invited to speak on infantry soldiers in the former Yugoslavia.

NATHAN FERGUSON

When I first joined the army, I had no idea what I was getting myself into. They started treating you nicely, made you feel comfortable but then when the bus finally stopped, after the 3 hour, 4-hour bus drive, you just had a bunch of soldiers in uniform who jumped and grabbed our equipment, began throwing them off the bus and started yelling at us and you then realize that you were in a different scenario. This is a lot more than what you expected. They indoctrinated you to what you are going to be facing.

The first two weeks were filled with cold showers and early wake ups. You had runs and Physical Training (PT) and they really try to weed out people that they felt didn't belong. It worked because people were quitting every day. The biggest challenge came after two weeks, we were told to run without our equipment in just our shorts and t-shirts. We should have known better because it was the hardest run that I ever did and I actually ran marathons. They did a combination run where different sergeant and corporals take turns running us but we had to continuously run but there had to have been 70 people and even more probably but at the end of the run. I counted only 7 people that had made the run. I looked over and all the women, there wasn't many there were about 9 women in total. However, I witnessed grown men stronger and much bigger than myself cried, I was only eighteen at the time. I have never seen grown men cry for any other reason. They were just beat. It's something, up to this day that I will always remember and this happened 21 years ago.

Yeah, that 2 months training, that was the big, big experience I had. Especially near in our last week of training there was a sleep deprivation exercise. It's consisted of 72-hour drill work where you are given minimum time to sleep and part of it is preparing you for war. You have to dig trenches. Myself and 3 other guys were very good at trench digging. When we had finished and we're sitting around and the captain told us "we're going to separate you and dig other people's trenches" and I had been put in a group that just come off break and I got a full experience of how your mind really plays you because I had to do 2 days straight of little to no sleep at all. I had missed my break and you are going through the motions and your mind is playing tricks on you.

You begin see things that aren't there and you really discover how weak you are, how strong you are in that moment and to me, 72 hours of sleep deprivation is the hardest thing I have ever experienced even to this day. It's just a different experience you have in the military. So when the training was done, they shipped us back to our regiment and we had to meet all the captains, the other soldiers. The whole summer, you were called a recruit, you couldn't call yourself a private because you hadn't earned the hook so we all knew that we had to finish the training to be accepted in the group and to see all the people that you will be serving with. It was really good but at the same time you are still a soldier.

You've been over there for 2 months, just constant training, no breaks, no days off. And to see people acting normally, it was different for you because you really were trained on just following the chain of command and looking out for your brother on the left and your brother on the right. It was a surreal experience to see these different soldiers, different ranks and they were treating you like you were one of them now and you knew you had something to achieve. You wanted to move up in rank. You wanted to learn different experiences. Except you still were in that soldier mentality.

When we had finished our training and before we were shipped back home, they did a graduation prayer for the soldiers at that time of my life, I wasn't too well connected with my family and you might have gotten 3 phone calls in the summer and I used one of my phone calls to call my sister, the only person that I really had a communication with. You could do letters but I phoned her and she promised me she'd be there to watch me graduate. Upon graduation there were a lot of people when I looked around. We got dismissed, everyone went running to their family getting hugs and I looked left and right and I couldn't see anyone. My sister ended up coming 2 hours later but I was overjoyed to see her realize I had accomplished something by having the opportunity to pass one of the hardest thing you could every experience. However, not getting to celebrate it with family or someone you love and getting to see everyone else getting hugs from their moms and sisters, wife, husband. It was a great feeling but a very lonely feeling at the same time.

During training exercises, you get to meet different soldiers, different people in charge. I had the opportunity to meet Corporal Salick during training and to look at him, you could see that he carried himself a little better than everyone else. There was a difference between the RCR soldiers and us from the regiments where we did soldiering and we got back to or regular lives, and they were complete soldiers but Cpl. Salick carried himself the way that you understood that you need to follow him and what he is going to tell you is good. He became to me, someone I look up to and I wanted to be around him because he was just quicker, stronger and faster than everyone else.

I can remember one moment when we were in Meaford and we were given a short break and a few of us started joking around. A Master Corporal from a different regiment came over and questioned us on why we were fooling around and why we were doing this and that. Of course we didn't speak back because he was a master corporal we were only privates. Corporal Salick had just gotten back and he said "don't worry, I had given them a break" and he tried to strong arm corporal Salick because he was a master corporal and corporal Salick didn't take to that at all. "these are my boys, we are having a break" and the master corporal realized that he wasn't dealing with just a "yes man" corporal. He ran to a sergeant to get some support trying to say that he outranks him and that he should listen but it was very impressionable to us privates to see a sergeant back the corporal instead of a master corporal. He too was from RCR and he understood that corporal Salick, even though he had a lower rank, he's still in charge. If a battle is taking place, the master corporal shouldn't be in charge it should be corporal Salick and that was proven right there as master corporal was sent away and corporal Salick was backed up.

So in training in Florida, we got sent there and it was a one-week training, we did a FIBUA (fighting in built-up areas), training and I believe it was called FIBUA which would be in tunnels. FIBUA training would be our final battle where they took a company of at least 100 people and we did a mock war and it was really a different experience because it's not play. It's not real but in our minds we were doing this for real. We had gear where they shoot blanks at you. If you're hit, the mils gear would make a sound and you're out of the war. And it was at least a 4-hour battle we did over a long stretch of land next to a building area. People were getting shot and they were getting killed throughout the village and at one moment we got all scattered up. I do remember corporal Salick running from behind to take lead and we continued the battle. This is where you really understand the chain of command. You follow the soldier with the higher rank.

There was a lieutenant that took us and told Corporal Salick he's in charge and get us to clear one side of a building and go to another side and people were still getting shot. By the end of the battle, it was cold and there was only 11 of us left. The lieutenant, corporal Salick and 9 other of us private or corporals. To see all the people and some were told, if you're shot, you lay down there and to see all the people laying down and you know how many people you started with and a few people were left, there's an impression on you, you understand that if you were on that one spot over there you could've been dead and you really appreciate what soldiers go through even though it was a little training exercise. At any moment you could be gone in a real situation of war.

To me, it's kind of funny how military experience started because I grew up in Flemingdon Park and it was a bad neighborhood especially at the time. I grew up where there were patty wagons parked by the government. You just grow up as a young guy and you want to live the life of the people around you. I made all the bad mistakes that all my friends did and I got myself in a little bit of trouble with the law. A friend of mine said, "let's join the military," I didn't know what it was. And I said "sure, let's go away for a couple of months" and in that time it took an 18-year-old boy and turned him into a man developing and learning real skills. Coming back, I no longer felt the need to hang out with those guys and follow what I thought was cool back then. I took advantage of every opportunity the military offered.

Thursday nights were given up when the military allowed us to do training. I went away as much as possible not to make money however to keep gaining knowledge and many different experiences. I really attribute my success now, near 40 with my wife where I am close to being a millionaire and I had zero dollars to my name when I started. I did not have anything to offer my children however my daughter has now finished university. Hence, none of this would be possible if I had lived my normal life in the streets. Everything I have today is because of the army.

Cpl Salick and Pte Onek Adyanga.

PTE. ADYANGA

Over the course of my studies at Trinity College, University of Toronto, I learned a great deal of the values that drive Canada's middle power internationalism on the global stage and grew to like it. Canada's peacekeeping role in trouble spots around the world gave many societies opportunity to deescalate conflict, and transform society from violence to civic coexistence. I greatly identified with the peacekeeping policy and wanted to contribute toward promoting it. Canada, and particularly the cosmopolitan city of Toronto, also greatly impressed me. In spite of its severe winters, there were many activities to participate in during winter and summer, if one is willing to give it a try. I joined many athletic activities, learned skating at Nathan Philip Square and at Habourfront Center, rode my bicycle during summers, attended concerts in the city, and had great fun at the many nightclubs around the city. The city was safe, vibrant, peaceful and multicultural. The love for Canada's peacekeeping role and the cosmopolitan city of Toronto grew over time that I wanted to contribute positively toward promoting it. The best approach to promote these values, I thought, was to join the Canadian army. But I had to wait until my successful completion of a Master of Arts degree in Political Science from the University of Toronto.

I enlisted in the fall of 1993, after taking the oath of military service at the Canadian Recruitment Center, located at the northwestern intersection of Yonge and Sheppard. Our cohorts were driven to Downsview army base to pick our kits. Returning to my apartment located at the intersection of Yonge and Sherbourne streets by a southbound subway, I labored with my military issued military equipment, ready to start my infantry training. I was given clear instructions: first, ensure that you get to your unit for training on Tuesday and Thursday evenings and to bring with me requisite clothing for induction. Second, arrive early to sort out administrative matters before the start of the induction program. Third, to report to my infantry unit, the Royal Regiment of Canada (RRC), located at Fort York Armories, near Exhibition Place on the shore of Lake Ontario.

My first experience at Fort York Armories was an exhilaration. I found that many military units were operating out of this same building. There were the ranger unit, communication unit, medical units, etc., as well as the Royal Regiment of Canada. I dutifully reported to my unit and was issued more military equipment for my training. Our training officers briefed and released us to the many non-commissioned members who would be our main instructor for the induction program. Among the many non-commissioned members was Cpl. Derek Abdul Salick.

We formed four lines and the first order of business was inspecting our kit to ensure that we have all of the required kits for training. We then reformed into groups to begin our induction training. We were given lectures on expectations of our role as soldiers, should we endure and succeed in our training. For several weeks, we were given lectures on various topics including chain of command, military code of conduct, rules of engagement, and obedience to the constitution and civil leadership of Canada. As I got to know many of my instructors, I realized that Corporal Salick was our main instructor. He was knowledgeable, treated us with professionalism and showed much enthusiasm in our induction. I grew to value his instruction that I took whatever he taught me with all the seriousness expected of a dedicated inductee.

The induction phase at Fort York Armories lasted several weeks of the winter months and transitioned to field training at Camp Borden. Camp Borden is the first proving ground for infantry trainees to learn in challenging field conditions. It is an area comprised of rolling hills, thick vegetation and forests, and series of rivulets draining into several small lakes of central Ontario. The several lakes moderate the climate that temperature variations over the course of the day if felt by everyone. We could have fairly warm days to very cold nights. For infantry training, the challenges of adapting to rapidly changing climatic conditions and terrain were great benefits to improving physical conditioning.

Our instructor, Corporal Salick, was a great soldier who knew of challenges to new inductees learning the skill of becoming professional soldiers. His advice often was to never take anything for granted and to be prepared for all eventualities. Corporal Salick instructed us in field craft and battle craft. We learned camouflage and concealment, movement under fire and other necessary maneuvers. He was very knowledgeable and taught by example. Some of our battle craft trainings took us through long night marches, trench digging, several sleepless nights, ambush and counter-ambush drills, fire control, escape and evasion techniques. During all of these training exercises, Corporal took his duties with such zeal and determination that he frequently supervised us throughout the night, responded promptly to our needs, which were many. I felt that Corporal Salick was training all over again, since he led by example and endured all of the vagaries of the infantry training with us. We, as infantry troops, in training trusted his leadership and relied on his every word to learn the skill of our new military trade. Because of Corporal Salick's high standards, we had to work twice as hard to fulfill all of the expectations required of a skilled infantry section.

When we are not out for field maneuvers, we were always on the firing range to master the use of infantry fighting weapons. Our range practice commences usually very early morning, rain or shine and we work throughout the day practicing weapon safety, proper firing techniques, clearing stoppages and resuming fire according to command. It was useful to learn to engage targets at distant and close range, using varying firing positions. I remember clearly the single-mindedness Corporal Salick invested in our training that at the end of our range practice, we felt very confident using our weapons in various challenging conditions. Most of the required weapon procedures came spontaneously during our brisk training exercises, giving us even more confidence in ourselves, in using our weapons and carrying through missions with high sense of efficiency. We easily qualified on using our weapons because of the mastery and commitment Corporal Salick. His philosophy of teaching by example greatly inspired us that we were fully prepared for our infantry phase three training at the Canadian Infantry Training Center at Petawawa, northern Ontario.

I took my phase two skills taught by Corporal Salick to Petawawa, and had no difficulty completing my infantry course lasting for about three months. Petawawa was full of high impact activity, high-energy instructors. I remember Sergeants Hapgood, Newcombe, Shaffer, Mulholland and many others who kept us busy for the most part of the summer. Their training in the various aspects of the infantry skills consolidated what Corporal Salick had already taught me. It was wonderful that I gained more proficiency from repetitions of the skills that already knew. In particular, I surprised many of my instructors with my skills of target acquisition and shooting. I was adept at breathing technique, trigger control and delivering rapid accurate fire at static and moving targets. It was second nature that I could hit targets with such ease and credit must go to Corporal Salick for his dedicated and inspirational training at Camp Borden.

We graduated and returned to the Royal Regiment of Canada, fully qualified and ready to take on new task as may be assigned. We also participated as a unit for a field exercise and training at Quantico, Virginia. I was glad to be place under the section leadership of Corporal Salick. At Quantico, we underwent rigorous training in Military Operations in Urban Terrain (MOUT) at a facility built specifically for that purpose. Military operations in urban terrain require discipline, good leadership, well-trained and professional soldiers, and we were it. We began the training by establishing a position close to the training facility. Though snowfall was heavy, we bivouacked outdoors and piquet our position for the night. What was a particularly challenging aspect of the training was crawling through deep, dark underground sewer drainage systems. Those soldiers who were claustrophobic found depth, darkness, tight spaces, and narrow corners to maneuver on your knees and leopard crawl in order to advance forward, terrifying. With occasional staccato of gunfire and relying on hearing in the dark recesses of the sewer networks to guess enemy positions, the nearly one-hour underground maneuver was as challenging as anything one could ever experience. Collectively as a team led by Corporal Salick, we made it through the sewer system with confidence and single-mindedness of purpose. After action debriefing, we then recommenced another round of exercise changing role of between assaulting and defending forces for most of the day. The experience was invaluable and it offered a different perspective to war in cities. It also reminded us of the laws of warfare learned during our phase two training at Fort York Armories.

The final day of our exercise was a culmination of all that we have exercised over the duration of the training. We went through the MOUT facility with ease, knowing every tactic of warfare in that terrain, and minimizing civilian casualties as we clear enemies out of rooms, buildings and area of exercise. With our American Marine Corps colleagues, we had a wonderful exchange of ideas, learned a lot from each other and built a common base of knowledge. It was a well worth exercise that I enjoyed and fondly reminisce still today. Corporal Salick was our section team leader and on the return flight aboard Hercules C130 aircraft to Trenton Air Base, near Kingston, Ontario, we enjoyed a discussion about our particular and unique set of lessons learned.

The next military exercise we went together on was dubbed Operation Southern Strike and it took place in Camp Blanding, Saint Augustine, Florida. Saint Augustine is a historic city, but fairly hot for the month of March. We flew out of Trenton Air Base and arrived later in the evening. Our field deployment was immediate: we loaded our vehicles, took out our weapons and drove out to the field arriving at dusk. As part of our standard operating procedure, we established our defensive position, dug trenches and proceeded to hanker down for the evening, while patrols went out immediately. The evening was quiet and uneventful. Morning began with moving to a new site where we would spend few days at a time until the climax of our exercise at Smithville village.

I was deployed with the vehicle mounted TOW2 missile group, while Corporal Salick was leading a section of infantrymen for the final assault on Smithville Village. Salick's section was located on our right and fast moving to join a firefight that we could hear very loudly. Coming fast on their heels, our mission was to provide support in case Salick's group meet armored resistance in breaching the perimeter of Smithville village. The day was hot, humid and full of engagements. Finally, we reached Smithville village after Salick and group had successfully secured it. We drove into Smithville, finding his unit busy removing obstacles, including barbwires to ease access and reorganization of the defensive lines.

CORPORAL SALICK

In 1994, while pursuing my degree at York and working with the 10/90 battalion (10% regular force and 90% reserves), I was offered an advanced leadership course (i.e., an Infantry Section Commander course (ISCC)) which commenced in the fall of that year. At the Meaford Training Centre (MTC), I met an exceptional human being and soldier, Robert Short. We blended into a cohesive group/section including myself, "Short," Richard, Thibault, Twaddle, and Wrattan. We were a section of seasoned soldiers. They had arrived straight from the Battalions in the field; they were keen, mature, professional soldiers. I recall that Rob was always there to lend support to anyone of the soldiers in the course; especially those from our section. His personality gave the impression of a consistently laid back, responsible family man. From September to December of that year we lived in the same space; we breathed the same air; worked for each other and dug the same trenches. I remember vividly the nights, when training was over with at midnight, we would be bellowing words of command across a parade square; giving each other drills; just to be perfect in everything that we did-the RCR way! "never pass a fault." This was our mantra.

Rob hailed from the East Coast, New Brunswick. When our course ended, we congratulated each other and I gave Rob a brotherly hug and thanked him for sharing his great knowledge with me and the other boys. As far as I am concerned, he is the epitome of the "soldier's soldier." When we parted, I said to him that I did not believe we will ever meet again and as we departed to our separate postings, wished him the best of luck with his family.

In January 1995, I am now instructing QL2 courses, also maintaining my responsibilities at a unit while pursuing my university degree. One of the highlights, meeting Prince Charles where I was given the opportunity to instruct precision drills for His Majesty. I was then invited to the officer's mess for a meet and greet session with the Prince in attendance.

At this time, I was aggressively attempting the impossible. I was taking 5 full courses at York University while serving the military, and to be honest, after completing my leadership course, my responsibilities at the unit grew. In fact, even though I was enjoying the challenges of working and studying full time, there were times when I questioned my decision to take on so much. But then, my military training helped me to endure. "Never let up! Take every opportunity life has to offer!" These were the ideas that set us apart from others. I completed most of my university courses at the end of the year, which was timely because, just two courses short of my B.A. Degree in Political Science, I received notice that I was to be posted to the Canadian Forces Base (CFB) in Petawawa, Ontario, Canada.

The years at RSS Toronto taught me how to be a better leader and that brought greater responsibilities. Then in 1996, my home unit 3RCR requested my service back to CFB Petawawa without hesitation I was there at the base to start again. Where? I learned that soldiers were needed for the next rotation to Bosnia. This was my dedication to my unit and the boys. I now had the ability to bench press 250 pounds ten times, harness a 50-pound rucksack and run 30 kilometers. I felt that the only way I could execute my job is by being the best of the best (however, as the old saying goes, "there is always someone better). My return to the unit was different this time, because there were so many new faces and very few old boys. The unit prepared and trained for a year before the tour. We needed this time to get ready because we now accepted militiamen to fill the shortages of our depleted manpower. It was critical in our training to have everyone working on the same page. We went through a very comprehensive training program before we left for Bosnia.

In addition to the physical conditioning, we were given several briefs on the history, language and culture of the people and handouts on the language and a few basic lessons so that we could communicate with the local people. Then, on July 15th 1998, we arrived in Bosnia Herzegovina, where our primary mission was to maintain a safe and secure environment within our Area of Responsibility (AOR); and our secondary role was to provide humanitarian aid whenever possible.

Chapter 3: Bosnia

On June 17th 1996, I arrived in Petawawa and experienced something akin to a family reunion. Most of the boys from my leadership course and a few members who were still serving from the late 1980's to the early 1990's were there. I soon found out that the unit was reorganizing and rebuilding in preparation for the next tour to Bosnia Herzegovina.

It was heart-warming to see my heroes again, and to my surprise, Rob Short. The moment he saw me, always cool and professional, with a huge smile and arms outstretched he stated "Slick! Welcome to 3RCR." But then we didn't have a lot of time to catch up on things. The build up to Bosnia went fast. A lot of new soldiers, in addition to the reservists would be deployed with us on this mission, which basically meant a lot more work was expected from the leaders and seasoned soldiers to have the team ready for the operation. In this period, I had as my section commander, Sgt. Wayne Evans.

Wayne was laid back and very professional, always assessing all situations and taking a cool approach to resolving them. He was an individual who ensured each and every soldier was good to go while on duty and in their personal lives (personal development). For example, he supported my goal of pursuing a university degree over a five-year period. He was always there to ensure that space was created where I could attend my classes. He also propelled me forward to get promoted for the upcoming tour which was in 2001. He always saw great potential in our team. He had an ability to bring soldiers from different backgrounds and abilities to come together to be a cohesive unit and to be victorious in every task assigned to us. I learned so much from Wayne, mostly his cool approach and his ability to deescalate situations.

Sergeant Evans' second in command was Mcpl. John Proulx. What was exceptional about Johnny, he picked up languages very easily. Therefore, he was fluent in English, French and Serbian-Croatian language. And the little German I knew while communicating to the locals, he actually picked up some of the German language. These two men, made sure our section was ready for any task, the boys, myself, Hancock, Lahey, Browne, Bohrson, and Crawford.

It was early January, we had been working together for the last 6 months in preparation for our tour to Bosnia, when the ice storm of 1998 occurred; it was a freak of nature. We the soldiers of 3RCR along with others were dispatched to Ottawa and Quebec. It was the largest deployment of Canadian troops since the Korean war, with 16,000 soldiers, 12,000 in Quebec, and 4,000 in Ontario. The damage to the trees and electrical infrastructure left millions of citizens in darkness. This went on from weeks to months. There was a complete shutdown of activities in Ottawa and Montreal. For many roads it was impossible to have a flow of traffic because of the heavy snow, fallen trees, broken power lines, and the heavy ice. The civilian emergency vehicles could not move.

The RCR boys started clearing the roads, rescuing people, and animals trapped by the storm, evacuating the sick, providing food and shelter, for roughly about 100,000 people who were frozen in and out of their homes. We had to ensure the farms had the fuel and generators required to keep their operations going.

It was amazing to see my heroes work, Evans, Proulx, Hancock, Lahey, Bohrson, Brown, Crawford, to see these guys in this element. It was very cold and they were working 24 hours, 7 days a week. This is what I call tremendous duty to one's nation. They were cutting trees into logs, removing them from the road, taking food and water to homes where people were trapped, creating access routes for movement in and out of some of these homes; I was in awe with the tremendous work ethic displayed by my heroes.

In the summer of 1998, the battalion was deployed to Bosnia Herzegovina. We landed in Zagreb, Croatia and then rode a bus to the most Northern section of Bosnia-Herzegovina, Velika Kladusa. As we entered Velika Kladusa in the wee hours of the morning, the air appeared still and heavy, the setting looked gloomy, little of life seemed to be happening. I felt as though we had much to do, and some of us will not make it back to Canada. But what can I say? This is our job, our life; we had signed the dotted line to give all to our Country. The first Bosnian tour!

It was a period in Bosnia where, in spite of a landscape disfigured by the ravages of war, people were attempting to install a democracy with a western twist. Our main responsibility was the City of Velika Kladusa. This was the most northern city of Bosnia next to Zagreb, Croatia. As I was a practicing Muslim, I requested permission to attend the local mosque on Fridays, which my command approved. This engagement I saw had an added feature of helping to build trust with the locals. Our patrols usually lasted eight hours; however, our team will be the QRF (Quick Reaction Force) either before or after our patrol. Therefore, technically we would be on the go for 16 hours, non-stop every 24 hours. I was ready for any physical opposition, it was important for us to respect the locals and work for them. From my years in Germany I had held on to parts of the German language, which assisted my patrols and my personal contact with the locals, quite a number of the locals spoke the German language. The reason for this, some actually worked in Germany and usually travel to and from between the two countries. On my foot patrols I never anticipated some of the scenes I witnessed. We went into areas where women were left beaten, battered, bruised and scared for their lives. They would relay their stories to us with an utter sense of defeat. I felt helpless because our arrival was a few years too late. Some of these young women (average age 24 years) would state that: "they are just waiting for death." The tone of hopelessness I heard in their voices tore at the very core of my being. Their living conditions, in half-blown homes, littered with the minimum living essentials of food, water and clothing, reeked of despair.

I must confess that I did not anticipate the horror that I encountered in these cities when we arrived. I came to the realization that, it did not matter how many guns I could carry, or how many miles I could run or how much weight I could lift, my training did not prepare me for what I saw, when I looked into the faces of these "casualties of war" that I met. How could I even begin to understand their pain and hurt? I would have liked to reassure them that I could solve their problems; this is what they seemed to be asking of me when I looked into their eyes. I will never forget the images that I saw there, and the words they said to me in desperation, it will torment me for the rest of my life. These days, I often ask, "what kind of men will participate in these hideous acts towards women? The nature and scope of the barbaric acts committed against women and children in the name of ethnic cleansing defeated understanding. I have many times tried to come to terms with this reality.

When WW2 ended in 1945 and leaders were chosen to rebuild their Yugoslavian countries, Josef Broz Tito was named president of Yugoslavia and he held onto that title up until his death in 1980. It is believed he ruled with an iron fist. "He will kill a thousand to save a million" was one of his philosophies, which created fear in many that allowed him to control the state successfully. The joining of six Republics created Yugoslavia: Slovenia, Croatia, Bosnia, Serbia, Montenegro and Macedonia. Tito believed and professed that all were Yugoslavian's and he did not care for sub-nationalism. Therefore, he attempted to create the melting pot theory. Later on in his career he eased off on Yugoslavia nationalism and pushed sub-nationalism for all except Bosnia and Albania. Within the Bosnia state the Serbs and Croatians were allowed to identify themselves, but the Muslims were not. This iron-fisted individual, many respected and loved him while a few opposed him. In 1980 he passed away and the Yugoslavian Empire had lost its stability.

"On that day we'll say to Hell: have you had enough? And Hell will answer: Is there more?" (Silber, 25)

Muslims crowd into trucks, run into the woods and some are shot dead trying to escape the Serbian attack. As Croatian soldiers advance, Serbian refugees flee in convoys or tractors.

The writer would like the reader not only to read, however visualize these events in Eastern Europe. Nations in the west and the mighty U.S.A became an observer to this human atrocity. Like an accident everyone stood around the scene and looked in. The Global North Nations profess to be leaders in democracy, but yet they did not do anything. Although we(Canadians) have a small army we were the first International Army to control the madness, however once again the UN failed my heroes. The world witnessed the Serbs and Croats annihilating the Muslims from different sides. Thereafter they were all doing it to each other. One must wonder, is this the price for so-called democracy, or was this a plan influenced by foreign powers to break up Yugoslavia. In truth it was a desire of one mad man (Slobodan Milosevic) to take control of Yugoslavia. It is believed that it was his lifelong dream to step into the shoes of Josef Broz Tito. The first Yugoslavia was born after WW1 when the Serbs, Croats and Slovenes merged their states into the kingdom of the Serbs, Croats and Slovenes. The second Yugoslavia rose from blood and tragedy, dust and ashes of WW2.

Former Yugoslavia up until 1991 was made up of six Republics that included: Slovenia, Serbia, Croatia, Macedonia, Montenegro Bosnia and Herzegovina. Also two autonomous provinces within Serbia, Kosovo and Vojvodina. They covered an area of 255,804 square kilometers in SE Europe. Bordered by Austria and Hungary on the north, Romania and Bulgaria on the east, Greece and Albania on the south and Italy on the west. This made up a population of 22 million people. The breaking up of Yugoslavia was created by nationalistic feelings by subcultures that consequently had an end result of interethnic hatred and violence.

In 1991 Slobodan Milosevic's dream seemed rather possible. This was his chance to show the world that he is not only as good, but also greater than Josef Broz Tito. With his J.N.A (Yugoslavian National Army) he attacked Slovenia because it was the richest republic. In the end, he failed. Many of his soldiers deserted because they thought it was unfair. His next move was to attack Croatia and after six days they had no gains so they withdrew. The reason for this was that President Tudjman stood up against him. In 1992 Croatia announced independence. Milosevic realized he had failed; Tudjman and Milosevic decided to separate Bosnia to create a Greater Serbia and a Greater Croatia through nationalistic propaganda. Simultaneously prior to the civil war, the Serbs, Croats and Muslims lived in Bosnia peacefully. They also had inter-religious marriages. Simultaneously one must acknowledge that they all came from a similar background. (Southern Slavs)

When propaganda messages are distributed to the ignorant masses this was the result. For 1200 days and nights, Croats and Serbs surrounded an area known as Bihac pocket. During the period of 92-95, 200,000 Muslims were placed in concentration camps and were annihilated. The Muslims fought back, although under armed and undermanned they started to push the Serbs and Croats out of their territory and had started to cover ground that belonged to Serbia and Croatia. The Muslims were informed by the U.N to stop their progress. Simultaneously after interviewing many local Muslims in that location they were quite proud because the pocket has never been defeated through its known history.

Some are wondering where did the Muslims get arms to defend themselves. The U.S.A and the G-7 PAC provided their military supplies for them. In 1998 we continued training with the young Muslim sons on small arms and using the 84mm weapon. Is it not better to teach them how to defend themselves with modern equipment, hence they can defend self and country?

Unfortunately, war and violence have had a long tradition in the Balkans. Many diverse cultures have clashed and blended into the ones that prevailed. Many invaders came, urged war and super imposed their cultures. Therefore, with different nations and cultures this created a diverse Yugoslavia, a world of its own, a combination of eastern and western culture, Turkish and European, Islamic and Christian influences.

UNDERSTANDING BOSNIA

> *Turning and turning in the widening gyre*
> *The falcon cannot hear the falconer;*
> *Things fall apart; the centre cannot hold;*
> *Mere anarchy is loosed upon the world,*
> *The blood-dimmed tide is loosed, and everywhere*
> *The ceremony of innocence is drowned;*
> *The best lack all conviction, while the worst*
> *Are full of passionate intensity.*
> *(From "The Second Coming"*
> *By William Butler Yeats)*

The end of the Cold War brought about a stark readjustment of international power structures. Where the Cold War era had been marked by spheres of influence, and battles fought by proxy through third world stand-ins for the United States and the USSR, the post-cold war era began not with a bang, but with a vacuum.

The sudden, and very much unforeseen collapse of Soviet communism, most dramatically marked by the fall of the Berlin Wall, happened too quickly for a stabilizing power structure to assert itself across the globe before, as Yeats might have said, things fell apart. In the decade and a half since that momentous time, a number of shocking conflicts have arisen in a number of areas around the world. Rwanda, Haiti, East Timor, Chechnya, Bosnia, and Somalia, all bring to mind chilly connotations of epic savagery, and the complete breakdown of human society. In some of these conflicts, poverty, underdevelopment, and environmental crises were key factors in the ensuing violence. In others, such as in the Rwandan conflict, the legacy of colonialism set the stage for genocide.

In the Balkans' wars, specifically in the Bosnian conflict, it was not poverty, underdevelopment, environmental crises, nor colonial legacy that could be pointed to as key causes of the conflict. In Bosnia, there were forces at play so deep, and so marked, that the entire conflict began with a sense of tragic inevitability. In Bosnia a maelstrom of ethnic violence was unleashed, requiring the efforts and intervention of a great many nations to enforce an uneasy peace. Though the events that occurred in Bosnia occurred between 92-95, they provide an extremely poignant window on the events of the present day. From the riots in Clichy-sous-Bois, to violent and ongoing worldwide protests over insulting depictions of the prophet Mohammed, ethnic tensions and vacillating leadership have begun to combine in a heady mix that echoes the possibility of a Bosnia redux, but on a much larger scale. I will illustrate how in the Bosnian conflict ethnic hatred, a weak central authority, and malicious leadership were the central causes.

In order to properly advance the above proposition, I will first outline the late history of Yugoslavia prior to the commencement of hostilities, examine how a weak central authority exacerbated separatist and expansionist tensions, and then how malicious leadership played the capping role in the ensuing chaos and bloodshed.

After the second World War, Josef Broz Tito, a power seeking communist dictator, and national war hero, was elected as the leader of Yugoslavia (Jenkins, 261). He took a disparate, war ravaged, and shattered Yugoslavia, and forged it into a new Yugoslavia. Under Tito, Yugoslavia experienced levels peace, and prosperity unknown in other parts of Eastern Europe. He used every means at his disposal and "shaped Yugoslav national policy." (Vukevich, 1994:479) As Denitch (1994) contends, "Yugoslavia had been arguably the most successful experiment in building a multinational federation in Europe since the Second World War" (Ibid: 1). While there were restrictions on individual freedoms, Yugoslavia was a stable society on track to becoming a fully developed nation. In order to make and preserve this relative peace and prosperity, Tito attended to religion and ethnic nationalism with an iron hand. He ruthlessly dealt with opposition, and those who voiced ethnic, or religious nationalist sentiments. As Silber and Little (1995) state:

> *"In his eternal battle to keep the nations on equal footing, Tito ruthlessly suppressed any expression of resurgent nationalism. Enforcing his doctrine of "Brotherhood and Unity," he carried out purges of Serbs, Croats and Muslim, Slovenes, Macedonians, and Albanians, balancing his repression of any one nation against the others"* (Ibid: 29).

Yugoslavia, as Vlajki (1999) states, "was a multinational state with hidden tensions between the federal republics" (Vlajki, 1999:91). Tito fully understood this, and also understood that the dominant nation within the confederacy, Serbia, if not kept in check, would try to seize power to the detriment of the other federal republics. Tensions were beginning to surface in the late seventies, but it was in 1980 when the Yugoslavian conflict truly began.

> *"[In] 1978, on the occasion of celebrating the centennial of the League of Prizen Albanian euphoria over the festivities soon turned into nationalist agitation, with illegal distribution of*

leaflets and open confrontations with the police. But the real trigger for the escalation of violence was the death of Tito in May 1980" (Ibid: 115).

Tito had feared an eventual push for Serbian hegemony. In the decade following Tito's death, the vast majority of Yugoslavian military officers were Serbian. Then, in 1991, Yugoslavia began a rapid disintegration, which began when Slovenia began a push for independence. As O'Ballance (1995) *states:*

"Two ethnic, separatist wars were fought against the Belgrade Federal authority. The 'Ten-Day War' in June 1991 gained sovereign independence for the Republic of Slovenia, and the longer one, from June to November that year, brought the same status to Croatia. The defeated Yugoslav National Army (JNA), now almost completely Serb in content, withdrew in ignominy from those two republics" (O'Ballance, 1995: vii).

Following the successful successions of Slovenia and Croatia, Macedonia and Bosnia-Herzegovina also began to demand independence. In Bosnia-Herzegovina a vicious three-sided ethnic war soon began, which was made worse by the withdrawal of the JNA. The JNA was responsible for the defense of Yugoslavia as a whole. While the JNA had a duty to protect Bosnia-Herzegovina, the withdrawal was an event planned and executed with the intent of leaving the area defenseless. According to Sloan (1998), "During this period, Croatia and Serbia held secret talks about carving up Bosnia-Herzegovina such that part of it would go to Croatia, and part to Serbia" (Ibid: 14). It was not long before words became actions.

From then on, Bosnia-Herzegovina was defenseless. While Serbian leaders still made claims to organizations such as the UN that they were interested in reunifying Yugoslavia, in reality, the intention was to bring about the creation of Greater Serbia. This was where the conflict really began, but as events soon began to show, the conditions were also ripe for an unparalleled orgy of violence, violence made all the more extreme by its ground in, deeply ingrained, ethno-religious hatreds.

Historically, when one nation enters into an expansionist phase, and embarks on wars of conquest, the wars are conflicts between national entities. In World War I and World War II, America, Britain, Germany, Russia, and other nations involved in the conflicts all maintained distinct allegiances. Even if that allegiance changed, as in the case of Italy in World War II, the change was clear and unequivocal. What marks the Bosnian conflict as differing from this pattern is the way in which neighbours, brothers, fathers, and sons would turn against each other (Seudetic, 1998: xxxiii). There were no clear lines of allegiance, sure knowledge of who the enemy was, and due to this, national identities were subsumed by ethno-religious identities. Also, as Vrcan (1998) states: Bosnia "exhibit[ed] conflicting potential of the religious factor to emerge with force into the open" (Seudetic, 1998:108). When the time came, that religious factor emerged with a vengeance. That such would happen was not entirely unforeseeable.

As stated previously, Tito had repressed nationalist and religious sentiments. In fact, "the Yugoslav government subjected the religious communities to an intense pressure and surveillance, even outright persecution, in the immediate post-World War II years" (Mojzes, 1998:81). The suppression of religion did not eliminate faith, but simply kept it bottled up. The different religions gravitated to their own distinct areas.

> *"What always made Bosnia specific was the often, tense interaction at the conjunction of two major religious worlds (Christian and Islamic) and three connecting faith communities (Muslim, Orthodox, and Catholic). None was in overall majority, but each had its own regions of predominance"* (Shenk,1998:102).

Unfortunately, "areas of predominance" did not mean homogeneity, an issue which became a key factor in the ethnic cleansing that occurred where majority populations in different areas later turned on minority ethnic communities.

> *Religion and ethnicity were very strongly linked in Bosnia. According to Denitch (1994), in Bosnia "[r]eligion [was] the most commonly used ethnic identifier" (Denitch, 1994:29). In fact, there were no real ethnic differences between Serbs and Croats, other than religion (Ibid ;). In an interview, the former president of Bosnia-Herzegovina, Alija Izetbegovic, told author Mark Thompson, "[O]ur concern is with all three million Muslims in Yugoslavia...Perhaps you from Europe cannot understand this, because for you Muslims are defined by their faith, whereas here they are in the first place a national group" (Thompson,1992:99).*

> *The ethno-religious identities of the various groups in the Bosnian conflict were so distinct and hardened that that it was relatively easy for malignant forces to manipulate those perceived differences, and exacerbate tensions. As Denitch relates, with the*

> use of the mass media, the central government was able to exacerbate racial tensions (Denitch, 1994:62).

Ethno-religious hatreds in Yugoslavia had an extremely long history, too long in fact for this section to relate properly. Suffice to say that ethno-religious identities were so solidly ingrained into the Yugoslavian psyche that even thirty-five years of earnest efforts by Tito to eliminate these sympathies and associations could not, in fact, eliminate them. When the strong hand of Josef Broz Tito slackened its grip on the nation upon his death, the proverbial genie was let out of the bottle.

Tito had been holding power for so long in Yugoslavia, and had been unforgiving enough of political opposition that there were few known players who could assume his role upon his death (Magas, 1993:80). Tito made the decision to pass power from autocratic hands to oligarchic ones by creating a collective leadership that was comprised of equal representation from the six main republics, and the two autonomous regions (Ibid). In addition, Tito established an Executive Bureau of the Yugoslavian Communist Party, and a special committee that would oversee the Yugoslavian constitution (Ibid). It was system of checks and balances that, Tito hoped, would keep Yugoslavia stable, and allow representation of the various ethno-religious groups in Yugoslavia. Unfortunately, things did not work out as planned.

Tito was the prototypical 'iron-handed dictator'. Though he was generally forward thinking, in some ways more closely resembling the Hobbesian notion of benevolent dictator than Stalinist oppressor. Tito's key flaw was his inability to appoint a true successor, and his greatest failure was the weakening of the Yugoslavian presidency.

> *"Wary of appointing a successor, Tito created a hopelessly inefficient inheritor of his mantle: the collective head of state which was to replace him was an eight-member presidency, comprising one representative from each of the six republics, and one from each of Serbia's two autonomous provinces, Vojvodina and Kosovo. The presidency of this body would rotate annually between its members. As head of state, of the eight member residency, that individual was also the commander-in-chief of the Army"* (Silber & Little, 1998:29).

Today the European Union uses this form of rotating presidency, shifting yearly to a different nation. But in a nation like Yugoslavia, so very rife with long pent up ethnic and religious tensions, it was a recipe for disaster. As Jenkins states, "Tito's regime did not survive him, but like Oliver Cromwell's, dissolved in anarchy after his death" (Ibid: 419). The anarchy took a while to come, but one man in particular - Slobodan Milosevic, speeded it along.

In a pitch perfect proof of Plato's assertion in The Republic, the people of Yugoslavia, at least the Serbians themselves, were the authors of their own demise. As Plato states: "Now aren't the people always in the habit of setting up one man as their special champion, nurturing him and making him great...and it's clear that when a tyrant arises, this special leadership is the sole root from which he sprouts" (cited in Michael, 2001:159)

Furthermore, in his speech Milosevic referenced events following Tito's death, which had upset and angered Kosovo Albanians. As Sloan (1998) states:

> "[T]he spark in the Yugoslav tinderbox proved to be the rise of ethnic nationalism. The phenomenon could be traced to 1981 when ethnic Albanians in Kosovo protested against the failure of Belgrade's economic policies to improve their living conditions...The anti-Serbian tone of the 1981 riots prompted the Serb minority to protest to the Yugoslav federal government that it was being discriminated against by the ethnic Albanian controlled Kosovo government. (Sloan, 1998:12)

Milosevic's success at gaining populist support was made evident when, in 1987, he ascended to the Serbian presidency. While he was not truly a nationalist, he was canny enough to sense political opportunity, and knew how to take advantage of it. His populist demagoguery was a "new strategy [that] mobilized traditional Serbian nationalism combined with loyalty to the party and to the regime in order to repress the demands of the Albanian majority in the province of Kosovo" (Denitch, 1994:60). As Denitch contends, "In the late 1980's, in the absence of a Tito or an institutional equivalent as a legitimate arbiter, it became much more difficult to deal with a popular populist nationalism" (Ibid; 55). Milosevic knew that nationalism was not going to go away, and used it to his advantage.

Though Milosevic was not yet the President of Yugoslavia, and only the President of Serbia, his connections to Yugoslavian military in effect gave him executive authority. At his urging the JNA attacked Slovenia, and then Croatia, which also had begun a push for independence. The attacks were unsuccessful. This, however, did not deter Milosevic. In 1990, Yugoslavia held its first multi-party elections in forty-five years (Sekelj 248). The elections were marked through voting along the lines of ethnic blocs, with parliamentary seats divided along ethnic lines (Seroka, 1992:181). Slobodan Milosevic, through his control of majority ethnic blocs, was elected leader of Yugoslavia (Sekelj, 1993: 248). Unburdened by any need to appear removed from the conflict, Milosevic turned his attention to Bosnia, intent that the peace process, and by extension Bosnian independence, should fail. In 1992, in an effort to fully undermine the peace process, Milosevic handpicked General Ratko Mladic to command the Bosnian Serb Army (Sudetic, 198:169). Mladic, later became responsible for several massacres, the likes of which had not been seen since the Second World War. Mladic's actions were the carrying out of official doctrines of the Bosnian Serb government, led by Radovan Karadzic, who in many ways was Milosevic's lieutenant. Karadzic advocated a policy of ethnic separation from which the infamous term "ethnic cleansing" was coined (Hockenos, 2003:140). This included the extermination of thousands of Muslims in Srebrenica (Ibid: 151). The conflict was eventually brought to a halt through the intervention of the United Nations Protection Force, led by Major General Lewis MacKenzie (MacKenzie, 193:97). The aftermath of the conflict left Yugoslavia shattered, and in ruins both physically and psychologically. With countless dead, and millions of displaced persons, the Bosnian conflict was a signal conflict of the 1990's.

The seeds of Yugoslavia's destruction had been sowed long before its final demise. The death of Tito brought about the end of a strong centralized authority, allowing long dormant ethnic hatred to resurface. The hatreds were given reign by the lack of control from the centre, but then exacerbated by the calculated and malicious actions of Slobodan Milosevic, the charismatic demagogue who rode a wave of Serbian nationalist sentiment, and dragged Yugoslavia into the "heart of darkness." Though the Bosnian conflict, and the larger Balkans conflagration has long past, the very elements that gave rise to the madness and bloodshed in that small corner of Eastern Europe are alive and well in the world at large today. Hopefully the lessons of the Balkans conflict will be heeded, preventing some future demagogue from repeating this bloody history, but on a more global scale.

Additionally, according to some authors, the Bosnian conflict has tended to be understood from either two schools of thought in the West. With one understanding the conflict as, "a case of aggression against a UN member, which had a tradition of multi-ethnic tolerance, by ultranationalist forces using genocide as an instrument of territorial conquest," requiring international intervention (Goldstein and Pevenhouse, 1997:517). In this particular school of thought there was a clear division between the "bad guys"—the Serbian leadership and the "good guys"—the Bosnian government and society, creating a discourse of aggressor-victim (Ibid; 517-518).

The opposing school of thought came to understand the conflict as a civil war of equals with no aggressor or victim, rather "warring factions," tending to accept the legitimacy of ethnic nationalism and autonomy over preservation of a multiethnic society (Ibid). Supporters of the aggressor-victim school of thought included a majority in the UN General Assembly, the Islamic Conference, and the Bosnian government; while the warring-factions school of thought was supported by the European Union, the great powers on the UN Security council (especially so Russia), and the Serbia (Ibid). In the opinion of the authors citing earlier work of Hoffmann (1994), responses to the conflict were lacking as, "in Bosnia, as in Ethiopia and Munich in the 1930s, 'the international community made the mistake of simultaneously pursuing two incompatible policies...' [similarly] because the warring-factions and aggressor-victim schools rest on different assumptions about the specific response patterns of Serb forces," thus exploration of triangular reciprocity would be beneficial.

According to Goldstein and Pevehouse's time-series analysis of the Bosnian conflict argues that much can be observed. Although they were writing from a post-conflict position there was still much disagreement surrounding the nature of the conflict and responses. Perspective from the West on the conflict tended to come from either of two opposing schools of thought—the aggressor-victim or the warring-factions, as such the two understandings produced distinctly different policy recommendations with regards to international intervention and cooperation, particularly on the situation of Serbian responses to various international actions.

At the same time Yerlan Isakov, in his Journal for the Study of Conflict (2010), points out that ethnic and political conflict is not a new phenomenon, while it may alarm the international community when conflicts evolved to a state where violence occurs— "including terrorism, atrocities, wars, ethnic cleansing, and genocide," conflict is not new (Isakov, 2010:122). An important and decisive component of the evolution of conflict to violence is psychological. Isakov suggests that in conflict, "group members act on the basis of the knowledge, images, attitudes, feelings, and emotions that they hold about the conflict; about their own past, present, and future as a group; and about the rival group...As such, it is the psychological elements in conflicts, which are very much so reliant on stereotyping and prejudice that are key to the evolution, maintenance, and management of violent conflict" (Ibid).

The conflict that took place in Bosnia from 1992-1995 was the culmination of many complex factors. Chronologically, beginning from the late 1980s, a first contributor was the economic crisis which hit Yugoslavia, which next lead into the dissolution of the Socialist Federal Republic of Yugoslavia. After the fall of the Yugoslav Federation came a divisionary period marked by the rise of nationalism, where "the rise of old-time religious sentiments instigated by traditional elites," occurred which would lead into the evolution of conflict on Bosnia. In this context three Bosnian ethnic groups— Muslims (Bosniaks), Serbs, and Croats that prior to the fall of Yugoslavia, had managed to live together despite difference; now all sought "self-determination and control of the territory" (Ibid: 123). Although the conflict in Bosnia has often been understood as an ethnic conflict, this is misleading according to Isavok as all three groups belonged to the same ethnic group—South Slav, speaking Serbo-Croatian; the difference lied in religion (Ibid:123-24).

The conflict in Bosnia has been popularly discussed and understood as one of ethnic conflict linked to fundamental difference between warring factions. For example, Isakov (2010) holds that there was much more to this conflict, importantly a psychological element not related to disagreements or contradictions related to, "real issues such as territories, self-determination, resources or trade" (Ibid: 122). Isakov's analysis of the Bosnia conflict as possessing a psychological element heavily dependent on stereotyping and prejudice in the evolution, maintenance, and management of the conflict offers important insight and understanding into how it came to be that large amounts of people and societies came to participate and condone actions which looking back can only be described as atrocious. Isakov points out that it is the existence of stereotyping and prejudice— psychological intergroup repertoire (Bar-Tal and Teichman, 2005) which are the, "essential aspects of intergroup relations, [and] are among the basic psychological determinants of conflicts (cited in Isakov, 2010:123).

With respect to psychological intergroup repertoire which Isakov speaks to, guided by the work of Bar-Tal and Teichman (2005), are political leaders whom wield much control over its creation and preservation. While although ethnic tension may be present prior to conflict, "ethnic wars are typically the result of political leaders using myths, symbols, and memories of the past to create fears that fuel these tensions and hostile relations," a kind of political manipulation used to incite violence (Ibid:125). Key to this manipulation is the national narrative—which, "their hero, the nation, as unique in suffering; ...depict[ing] the national narratives of rival nations as illegitimate"

(Ibid 125). Psychological intergroup repertoire is usually provoked by a political leader and the use of the national narrative, it endures via the mass media and other social communication channels, which endorse stereotyping and prejudice though the spread of propaganda for example in education (Ibid: 127).

Following the Cold War there was a shift in conflict from East-West tensions to civil and ethno-religions clashes, as examples in Haiti, Afghanistan, the Balkans, and sub-Saharan Africa following the end of the Cold War (Gibbs, 2009:1). It was in this new post-Cold War conflict shift that humanitarian intervention would emerge and gain popular support, with the assumption that intervention on the part of the world's major powers would act as a deterrent for future conflict (Ibid). However, according to Gibbs, in the Yugoslav case, "external intervention was one of the principle causes of the conflict (Ibid). For Gibbs (2009),

> *"Interventions helped to trigger the breakup of Yugoslavia and the various wars that followed the breakup; later intervention served to intensify the war, and to spread the fighting. External intervention did not resolve or attenuate the conflict; it helped create the conflict in the first place"* (Gibbs, 2009:1-2).

Humanitarian interventionism is based on the premise that human rights take precedent over the rights of states and governments, which would put such an approach in conflict with the notion of territorial integrity which has historically guided international intervention, which has tended to place state sovereignty above human rights. This type of intervention while seeming straightforward is in actuality complex, as it relies on identifying an aggressor and a victim, which at times it not clear-cut, for example, "where both sides (or sometimes multiple) engage in cycles of atrocity and vengeance" (Ibid).

Thus, humanitarian intervention offers itself as a means for which outside powers can intervene in the sovereignty of a state without it being viewed as an act of war or aggression. As such humanitarian intervention bares much responsibility on the part of the intervening party to not seek ulterior motives, as humanitarianism can be used, "as a pretext to justify aggressive actions that serve to advance its economic and geostrategic position in the world" (Ibid 11). It is this motivation of humanitarian intervention that Gibbs comes to issue with, arguing, "acts of humanitarian intervention in Yugoslavia were perfectly consistent with the geo-strategic interest of the United States and other key states" (Ibid: 11).

MY HUMANITY

"WAR, there is no life like it. there is no life in it." Anonymous.

Bosnia, once a beautiful, peaceful, and prosperous region, has since become synonymous with death, suffering, terror, and destruction. Between, 1992 –1995 there was a descent into madness. It was in this place, and in this time that, as Yeats might say "things fell apart." The madness continued, unabated, until the international community could no longer ignore what was occurring. The reasons for the conflict seemed to stem from numerous interconnecting streams of development. It was at that time, in 1995, when the UN/NATO intervention troops arrived in Bosnia with true force, bringing, for the first time in that troubled country, real peace.

I will demonstrate that the UN/NATO intervention in the Balkan conflict in 1995 satisfied the requirements of a just war. To that end, I will discuss the idea "just war" as a theoretical construct, and along the way examine the history of the Balkan conflict, the effects of the conflict, as well as the UN/NATO intervention in the form of SFOR, and why the UN/NATO intervention can be called a just war.

The question as to what constitutes a just war is one that has been asked and debated for many centuries; but it is one that seems to have many different answers. In the end, the answer is a combination of five principles. To wage a just war you have to have just cause. Having just cause, the war has to then be pursued by a legitimate authority, and should be pursued only if the authority has the right intention. Next, there has to be a good chance of success, because engaging in a hopeless fight is not considered morally defensible. Finally, the war is just only if the achieved end was proportional to the means that were used. Once you satisfy these principles, only then can a conflict properly be called just.

At the end of the Second World War, Josef Broz Tito, a half-Slovene, half-Croat Communist Dictator, seized the reins of power and forced a chaotic group of entities known as the Balkans into a unified state that became the modern Yugoslavia. During Tito's reign, there was peace, and there was prosperity. While there may have been less of the freedoms that most Westerners are accustomed to, it was a far better place then, than it has become today. Tito did not allow any ethnic nationalism to rise or remain. He was ruthless in purging any nationalists who raised their voices. As Laura Silber and Allan Little state, in their book The Death of Yugoslavia:

"In his eternal battle to keep the nations on equal footing, Tito ruthlessly suppressed any expression of resurgent nationalism. Enforcing his doctrine of 'Brotherhood and Unity,' he carried out purges of Serbs, Croats and Muslim, Slovenes, Macedonians, and Albanians, balancing his repression of any one nation against the others" (Silber & Little, 1995:29).

Tito wanted to prevent history from repeating itself, where the dominant nation within the confederacy, the Serbs, would seize power to the detriment of the other nations. As the Serbs were twice as numerous as any other group, this was a distinct possibility. Tito, like all men, was merely mortal. Unable to appoint a successor with the same strength of will and vision as he had, his death brought an end to his dream of a unified Yugoslavia. He left in his place a weak willed and incapable system that did not have the ability to control the country as he had. In fact:

> *"Wary of appointing a successor, Tito created a hopelessly inefficient inheritor of his mantle: the collective head of state which was to replace him was an eight-member presidency, comprising one representative from each of the six republics, and one from each of Serbia's two autonomous provinces, Vojvodina and Kosovo. The presidency of this body would rotate annually between its members. As head of state, the eight-member presidency was also commander-in-chief of the Army"* (Ibid).

Perhaps in Tito's time this form of Government may have seemed democratic, equal, and balanced, but today one can only see the seeds of destruction that had been sown (especially) by his later decisions. Slobodan Milosevic, who is today a reviled war criminal, and whose name has become synonymous with that of other reviled dictators such as Hitler, Stalin, Pinochet, and Pol Pot, was a member in the eight-member presidency that succeeded Tito after his death in 1980. Then in 1987, Milosevic became the President of Serbia, and the true leader of the Serb nation, after a series of events that set the stage for the ethnic conflicts that were to come. Shortly after Tito's death, the nationalist fervor which Tito had suppressed so ruthlessly had begun to emerge again. Canny and young, Milosevic used these developments to catapult himself to the very top position in the country.

What is significant about Milosevic's commitments, especially when compared with Tito's, is the quality of his intentions. Simply put, Milosevic focused on the compartmentalization of power where Serbs would remain distinct form other ethnicities. Tito believed this kind of power that came with a unified body of ethnicities. This divergence in perspectives is critical in understanding much of the horrors that happened when Milosevic took over Tito's position. But, even so, the personalities of these leaders and the decisions they made must be assessed within the context of the realities of Yugoslavia at the time. For one thing, Tito had always feared the possibility of a surging Serbian hegemony, one that would subsume all other groups within Yugoslavia. After all, 90% of the officers of the Yugoslavian military were Serbian. This was the kind of potential that Tito was always aware of and managed, during his leadership, to keep in check.

On the other hand, Milosevic was only interested in Serbian hegemony: without, it is safe to add here, many of the nationalistic overtones that came later. I repeat. At the time Milosevic assumed the top position in the Serbian Communist party, given that he was not truly as nationalist as many of his supporters, he knew the political power they conferred and was more than willing to use it. As history would show, he was able to "seize the moment" when circumstances changed in Yugoslavia sometime after Tito died.

In 1991, Yugoslavia began a rapid disintegration, which actually started when Slovenia began a push for independence. At the time, Milosevic was not the President of Yugoslavia, just the President of Serbia, but his ethnic ties to the leadership of the Yugoslavian military gave him the power of command and control. At his urging, the JNA, which represented Yugoslavia's National Army, attacked Slovenia, and then Croatia, which had also begun a push for independence. However, the JNA was unsuccessful in preventing these countries from gaining political autonomy:

> "Two ethnic, separatist wars were fought against the Belgrade Federal authority. The 'Ten-Day War' in June 1991 gained sovereign independence for the Republic of Slovenia, and the longer one, from June to November that year, brought the same status to Croatia. The defeated Yugoslav National Army (JNA), now almost completely Serb in content, withdrew in ignominy from those two republics" (O'Ballance, 1995: P.vii).

Following the successful withdrawals of Slovenia and Croatia from Yugoslavia, in 1992 Macedonia and Bosnia-Herzegovina also began to demand independence. Bosnia-Herzegovina soon began drawing the attention of the world as a vicious three-sided ethnic war began, which escalated after the withdrawal of the JNA. The JNA was a body that was responsible for the defense of Yugoslavia as a whole, that is, all six states equally. Their withdrawal, an event which was planned and whose consequences were known, left the area, especially more vulnerable places like Bosnia-Herzegovina, defenseless to the encroachments of both single states and others who had begun to form new alliances in the region. For example: "During this period, Croatia and Serbia held secret talks about carving up Bosnia-Herzegovina such that part of it would go to Croatia, and part to Serbia" (Sloan, 1998: P.14).

From that point on, Bosnia-Herzegovina was left open for an attack by Serbian or Croatian nationalists. At this point, the now almost purely Serbian Yugoslavia, dropped its claim of attempting to recreate Yugoslavia. While Serbian leaders still repeated this claim to organizations such as the UN, in reality the drive to create a Greater Serbia was in full force. At this point, where the march of history appears to meet the present day, the effects of this unfolding drama explodes to become starkly apparent to those in the region and the world at large.

THE IMPACT OF CONFLICT

Thanks to the media, and its unending quest to document the tragedy and suffering of others in order to fill space in the newspapers and on television, what happened next in Bosnia-Herzegovina, is pretty well known. Day by day the world saw pictures of the siege of Sarajevo, evidence of ethnic cleansing, and an unending cycle of violence and hatred. From the perspective of the average viewer, the violence may have seemed random and chaotic; but, in reality it had chillingly clinical overtones: "The vicious three-sided civil war, dominated by a siege-and-starvation strategy and involving ethnic cleansing, detention camps, atrocities and hordes of refugees, dragged on month after month, as neither faction could raise sufficient military force to defeat the others" (O'Ballance, 1995: P.ix).

Each side knew what it wanted, and initiated actions in order to affect that end. The goal of each party was to remove the others from the area, to make it ethnically pure. The scope of violence was vast. It was not a military war where the only involved parties were those under arms; it was a total war where the tactics employed were everything from the regular use of force, to the psychological violence of rape, and the mass murder of non-combatants. The examples are myriad: "Muslim refugees run into the woods, crowd into trucks, some are shot dead while trying to escape a Serb onslaught. Serb refugees form endless convoys of tractors, fleeing a Croatian advance" (Silber and Little, 1995:25). As "[a] common practice for Serbian forces after occupying an area is that they will get rid of all non-Serbians to profess that the area solely belongs to Serbia...it is believed that 2.3 million people were displaced during the war years from 1992 – 1995" (Stigimayer, 1994:187).

As atrocity built upon atrocity, and as revenge was met by revenge, a point was long since crossed where any hope of a normal solution to the problem could be found. The UN, still unsure of its status, whether to be a observer or an interventionist, sat still as the violence continued. Philip Corwin, in his book Dubious Mandate: A Memoir of the UN in Bosnia, summer 1995, tells the story of the incident which became a key impetus for the UN/NATO intervention that shortly followed. In his journal entry for July 12, 1995, Corwin states: "Srebrenica fell during our trip back from GornjiVakuf. Forty thousand Moslems were trapped there. The Dutch troops were in Potocari, their base in the enclave, but they were powerless" (Corwin, 1999:210)

The numbers vary; 8000 Muslim men and young boys were trapped in Srebrenica, and had no way out. The Serbian General Mladic was promising that there won't be any slaughter; however, he was not fully believed. It seems as if nobody would help. In desperation, the Muslim authorities in Srebrenica appealed to the UN to help them, to either get them out of there, or establish a safe zone. But this did not happen. Soon the killing commenced. Some tried to run, to head for the hills, but were shot down. With the exception of a few who were lucky enough to get away, the Muslims of Srebrenica were slaughtered. Other sources had different figures and that those who were massacred. It wasn't as bad because the women and children were supposedly trucked to a different location but they never reached their destination.

In the aftermath of this event, made known to the world through the broadcast media, UNPROFOR, the UN force currently in Bosnia-Herzegovina, lost all credibility. A new mandate was required, and a new intervention was needed. This led to the creation of a UN/NATO force termed IFOR (Implementation Force), which later became known as the SFOR (Stabilization Force): "The humiliation of UN Peacekeepers chained to a lamp post or military installations...the fall of Srebrenica and Zipa, the fall of Krajina and the mass murder of Muslims, brought international effort to end the war" (Silber and Little, 1995: P. 364).

Compared with the previous years of relative complacency by UNPROFOR, IFOR came in hard and fast. Driven by the power of the media, and its ability to influence public opinion, Western leaders knew that action was required, and required immediately. In the court of public opinion, anything less would have meant culpability for future atrocities. At this moment the human atrocities witnessed by the civilized world was clearly overbearing. This led to a shift in attitude and military conduct.

SFOR AND THE *UN/NATO* INTERVENTION

On August 30th, 1995, at 0200 hours, IFOR began its attack on Serbian positions in Sarajevo and areas in Serbia itself. This was initiated in order to compel the Serbian forces to withdraw, and to force the opening of peace negotiations. Operation Deliberate Force (ODF) continued for sixteen days until a humbled Milosevic was forced to discuss peace, at which point, in September 1995, President Clinton initiated the Dayton Peace Accords. It was Clinton's skills as a mediator, in initiating this round of conflict resolution, which set the groundwork for the eventual peace as established by SFOR.

The IFOR initiative lasted for one year. For the most part, the UN/NATO bombardments ceased at the start of the Dayton Peace accords. With a mandate that called for the use of force to create peace, IFOR began its ground intervention. City, by town, by village, they secured the areas, and created a safe zone for the people who had remained. When most of the ground occupation was complete, IFOR was renamed SFOR, with a slightly modified mandate. SFOR started their mission in 1997 and continues to our present day. Military troops were in Bosnia to enforce the Dayton accord. As IFOR, the mandate was simply to use force in order to defend self and other non-combatants, but when the transition to SFOR was made, this changed: "SFOR's mission was to provide a secure and stable environment in which the Bosnians themselves, [that is] with assistance from international civilian groups, could rebuild their nation" (Daalder, 1997:10).

The 3RCR battle group's role were as follows: (1) to provide a safe and secure environment for the locals and self. (2) To provide humanitarian aid when it is necessary (Author's -Mcpl. Salick 3RCR Battle group, O coy., section 2i/c-recollection of how his role developed in the conflict). In addition, the actions of the emergent UN mandated body SFOR: 1) patrolling built up areas and borders for twenty-four hours a day, seven days a week; 2) cordoning off and searching houses for weapons; 3) escorting displaced persons back to their homes; 4) offering humanitarian aid where possible; 5) offering support and security for international NGO's who entered the affected areas. As the name implies, the goal was to now stabilize and help rebuild a shattered nation. This seeming paradox of war sometimes befuddles civilians. Through the use of force, IFOR was able to force the opposing sides apart. Then, as SFOR, they were able to create the environment where actual help could arrive, and the process of recovery could begin. By securing contested areas, and ensuring safe zones, SFOR was able to give international aid organizations and NGO's the environment they needed to begin the real work of humanitarian intervention. And it was real work that was needed, for at that point, not much of Bosnia was left:

> *"When the war ended, more than half of Bosnia's 4.3 million citizens had been displaced, either as refugees in host countries (1.2 million), or internally displaced persons within Bosnia's external border (1 million); roughly 250,000 were estimated dead or missing, communicable diseases increased two – fivefold, and physical and economic losses were severe. Destroyed assets were estimated by the World Bank at 15 – 20 Billion, industrial production reduced to 5 – 10%, 80% of agricultural equipment was destroyed, between 2-4 million land mines littered the country, coal production reduced by 90%, transportation, telecommunication, educational and health infrastructures were heavily damaged, and more than half of the country's housing stock was either destroyed or unusable. At the end of the war, unemployment reached 90%, and per capita GDP dropped by ¾"* (Cousens and Carter, 2001:2)

Notwithstanding, with the SFOR firmly in control, civilian groups were now safe and free to enter the area, and initiate humanitarian efforts. The UN/NATO intervention as an example of a just war, can be viewed between 1992 to August 1995, internal conflict in the Balkans escalated to the point where the violence was too much for the world community to take. There were daily reports in the world media of tens and then hundreds of thousands of refugees. There were reports of countless atrocities, some of which were rumoured to be like atrocities perpetrated in the holocaust. Diplomatic solutions to the conflict routinely failed. Economic sanctions did not seem to harm the combatants, but only exacerbated the suffering of the non-combatants, and the cycle of violence was escalating to seemingly unstoppable levels. According to the principles of just war theory, the UN/NATO intervention was undeniably just. First, there was just cause. Nations bordering the former Yugoslavia were strained to the breaking point with refugees fleeing the conflict. The end result of this would have meant a humanitarian crisis that would have drawn in more and more nations as the situation worsened. The media reports of possible mass graves, concentration camps, and ethnic cleansing brought to mind the principles of the Nuremberg Tribunal. The echoes of "never again" could be heard in newspapers, on television, and in the public discourse. Remaining uninvolved and neutral to the conflict was not a morally defensible position. Second, the war was pursued by an undeniably legitimate authority that the UN/NATO represented.

The United Nations sanctioned the intervention, which was enacted by NATO forces. The UN/NATO forces waded into the conflict in the hopes of ceasing the violence, so that civilized society could begin to function again. This was the right intention. It was not an invasion, it was not for the purposes of economic gain, but was enacted to bring hope to a hopeless situation. Further, this intervention had every chance of success. The combined military might of the NATO forces was fully capable of engaging the warring factions in Bosnia, using the force necessary to ensure the cessation of hostilities.

The final requirement of just war, that the ends were proportional to the means used, is perhaps the easiest to argue. Considering the situation at the time of the intervention, the means used were remarkably restrained. With the prevalence of ethnic cleansing by different factions and the perpetration of war crimes of all different kinds, from rape to murder to torture, a more drastic response could very well have been warranted. NATO used precision bombing to take out specified targets. Ground forces were used to secure areas to ensure the cessation of hostilities, and were not used to enact punitive measures or wage an indiscriminate war of retaliation. In the end, SFOR succeeded in accomplishing its objectives, making the UN/NATO intervention not only successful, but also remarkably restrained.

The history of the conflict in Bosnia-Herzegovina, with the slow build-up of ethnic tensions over the period of a decade, combined with an economic collapse and an unstable governmental framework, all set the stage for the violence that followed. When the real violence commenced, it was so ferocious and so fierce that simply asking the various sides to just forgive and forget would have been be naïve, foolish, and futile. This is essentially why UNPROFOR failed –because of weak leadership and the lack of a confirmed mission statement. When the slaughter in Srebrenica commenced, a Canadian Master Corporal, John Proulx (3rd RCR) stated: "We informed higher [The command post] of the massacre that was occurring, and we were ordered to go into Srebrenica and escort the UN delegates out" (Author's personal recollections). In ignoring the plight of the victims, and by only rendering assistance to its own members, the UN and the UNPROFOR failed in the most profound way. By standing aside, observing, forcing its soldiers to just watch the events unfolding, the UN acted as an accessory to the atrocities, and lost the moral foundation upon which their credibility rested. Because of this, the international community had to take matters into its own hands. The time of equivocation, and deliberation, as the UN was so good at doing, was over. It was time for a real intervention. At this point Just War theory applied, and the intervention, as well as the occupation had the full force of moral authority. Because there were so few casualties in comparison to the size of the intervention, and that the military objectives were fought with a humanitarian purpose in mind is what makes this intervention not only an example of a just war, however an exemplar of just war.

Simultaneously Sgt. Wayne Evans recalls on a latter tour to Bosnia. He was working with Dutch soldiers and they relayed to him that one of the Dutch officers committed suicide in Holland, who was in Srebrenica and failed to protect the Muslims, no doubt that will torment him forever, therefore, he committed suicide.

This map demonstrates the Dayton Accord 1995; the peace borders of Former Yugoslavia. This is when Stabilization Forces (S4) Eastern Europe, went to make a difference in the lives of the people of Bosnia. 'Ethnic cleansing' "Civilians, especially women and children, are the real casualties of War" Theo Morris.

PATROLS

Our "peacekeeping" role in the conflict, though interesting, is far too sterile a description of the reality of Bosnia when we were there. To put it mildly, dealing with the hatred that neighbours felt for each other was not just a matter of getting two people to drink a beer together. The hatred these people felt for each other was deep and immovable; one felt an animosity that burned as bright as the sun. It would have been easy to give up hope in these circumstances. However, if the truth be told, what the peacekeepers achieved in Bosnia was nothing short of spectacular. To have a better understanding of peacekeeping in Bosnia, starting with my own experiences, we will view some of the stories of infantry soldiers on the ground.

By 1998, SFOR was spread across Bosnia Herzegovina. In our Area of Responsibility (the Canadian Contingent), it appears that a greater part of the population had difficulty in understanding our role, as they watch us walking around carrying weapons.

www.nato.int/sfor/nations/canadian/b981210p.htm

A young man asked me, "Are you gunslingers, walking big and mighty in my country?" I replied, "We are only here to protect you and make sure that you grow up to be a man." We would try our utmost to maintain peace and create stability, so that this war-ridden and politically unstable country can move forward. The need for an economic base is evident. Factors that entrepreneurs can look at: the labour is cheap, people are hardworking, and there is lots of land available for production. The writer claims, "Of all countries I have travelled to date, the women are very hardworking here, there isn't any comparison. The people are very humble, less informed and can be easily coaxed into believing whatever doctrine the entrepreneurs will present to them.

Bosnia is moving away from the socialist type of Government to a Social-Democratic type of Government. The entrepreneurs are scared of entering Bosnia because of the political scene, which has created instability nation-wide. When one can be indoctrinated to kill his own brother because he does not share similar political views, then this exemplifies the extent of education in this country. The SDA is a party for mature folks, those with a bit of autonomy and is believed to be more Islamic than the other party (DNZ). The DNZ is a party that the majority of the young people will respond to, though not understanding the political scene, but can feel the injustices – people beaten up, broken limbs – and the local people will not do anything about the unfairness in society rich and poor, believers of Islam and non-believers. There are a few more political parties which presents to one's intellect initially that this is a democratic country but these small parties act as pressure groups (small groups influence political scene constantly). To sum up the political scene in one sentence, "The politicians are like prostitutes," as a religious leader stated to me with a stern and sad look on his face. Politicians easily sell themselves out to the highest bidder.

The Islamic religion entered Bosnia during the reign of Ottoman Turks and they possess remnants of that culture along with a Hungarian culture. However, Islam appears dominant today. One must mention that most religions have been practiced in the past for an individual or group's benefit. When looking at the Koran and the way of life that has been presented, to view the lifestyle of a large number of people living in Bosnia, Islam is different in Europe compared to the Middle East because the people have a modern lifestyle. The majority of the older generation follow Islam, while the younger generation is influenced by the media, and through their experiences of living and working in other countries in Europe and Scandinavian countries.

In this society education and sports appear to be a luxury for those who can afford it. In order for my young brother Moyen to reach the top, he must obtain a better education, determination and stay focused while training for football; this will enable him to beat the hand that life has dealt him. From the writer's observation, great men can come from such humble intellectual and physical beginnings, such as Abraham Lincoln, who was self-educated and became the U.S.

President in 1864. Another example is Pele, Brazilian football star, who played in three world cups and today he is the ambassador of football for his country. Therefore, the writer wishes the best for young Moyen and as stated before, whatever little we can do to see this young man win in life we will give him our fullest support.

Richard crouching down, this picture was taken in Bosnia sometime in December 1998.

Private Richard Moreno:

My name is Richard Moreno, there was a time I served in the military where I was with 3 RCR who were deployed to Bosnia for a 6-month peacekeeping Tour in July 1998 through to January 1999. Prior to being deployed, we were told that we would be spending the first three months at one camp and the last three at another. So for the first three months, the platoon was in Velika Kladusa, and the last three months in Coralici.

The kind of work that we were doing over there was patrolling the streets, helping out families that were affected by the war that occurred a few years before, and helping to keep the peace. We patrolled many areas during the day and even at night. Usually on a patrol there would be 6 soldiers and the translator and away we go. As much as the patrols were repetitive, there are only so few patrols that I will always remember because of the situation that occurred.

One day in August (just after a month being there) around 5 o'clock in the afternoon we were on our way back to camp and we were about 45 minutes away from the camp. As we were making our way back, there was a truck driving coming to our direction and I mention to the driver to slow down a little bit because it doesn't look like this guy in front of us is going to slow down. Just as we were passing him by, the driver swerved to avoid hitting us and instead hits a cow, the cow flies about 15-20 feet, with the owner holding on and the cow hits the corner part of the house landing on the owner's legs keeping him trapped there. This situation ended sadly for the cow. My section commander asked me if I saw what happened and as I replied yes, he said to write everything down of what I saw in my notepad because I am going to be asked a few more times in the next little while. Our Military Police showed up and asked what I saw, Interpol asked me the same questions, and then the Bosnian Police last. Eventually one of these officers told me that the other driver was saying that it was our fault and that we were going too fast. We didn't make it back to camp till closer to midnight.

Another time I remember perfectly well was this one day in September, we were going to pull vehicles over and do vehicle checks. The first car that I was told to pull over and it was the person that was wanted by police except this day he was travelling with his family. This person was like the Al Capone of Bosnia and his nickname that we had for him was "The Iguana." We were told that when he travels with his family he doesn't carry any types of weapons, however when he is by himself he is known to carry a few guns and harass families and taunt them to get money and other valuables that he can. My fire-team partner and I were tasked to keep an eye on him, while a couple of the other soldiers were searching the vehicle. The Iguana was trying to mess with our heads by pulling at the end of the barrel of my C-7 and my buddy's also, I yelled out "STOY" (stop in Bosnian), he didn't want to listen and tried doing it again, so I asked my section commander if I can let out a warning shot, of course he said no, I yelled to the translator and told him if he does that again there will be a warning shot. The translator told him to stop and sure enough the iguana stopped and a few more minutes later and the guys who were searching the vehicle came up empty handed. It was too bad because he was a wanted man and the only way to detain him would have been if he had a gun on him but instead we had to let him go.

One of the last memories I have took place sometime in December in which we were tasked to stay out at this area for like 3 days. This area was a small village, it looked abandoned because like the other areas we have seen, there were bullet holes everywhere around the houses. In this area there was only about 8 - 10 people living there. In this little village there were these hills and beyond the hills was a crossing point or border into Serbia. There were people coming and going through this border, some people were getting away from Serbia and some were leaving Bosnia to go into Serbia. It caused quite the conflict because even though there were border agents in place, there was some gun fire before we arrived.

CORPORAL BEN BROWNE/SLICK 1998

We did a lot of vehicle patrols in Velika Kladusa as they were preparing for elections. We went down to the Croatian border, then on our way back, it was about 0200 hours/2am, we stopped at the DNZ headquarters where we decided to take a 5-minute rest, have some rations. All of the sudden a rocket launcher smashes into the wall above our heads. Box lunches close, and we turn on our power lights (mounted on our vehicle), into the area where the round came from. However, in no man's land we could not find the culprits.

While on a vehicle patrol, we heard over the radio that shots were fired at the castle, hence, we immediately made our way there. We conducted a thorough search of the castle and without any luck, there was no one to be found. However, we were now preparing to leave the castle and suddenly a shot was fired grazing the helmet of one of the boys. I pulled the vehicle into a gully (a makeshift driveway in the mountain), and we turned our power light on. After 10 minutes we could not locate the bastards/culprits.

A high official in Velika Kladusa's son was getting married, we were summoned to do security for the wedding because there is always an imminent threat as they were all Muslims. They were opposing each other because of political differences. Our mission was to maintain peace at the wedding.

I remember while we were patrolling on New Year's Eve, everything was quiet, all shops closed, and suddenly a group of young people saw us patrolling and invited us into their home to ring in the New Year. Corporal Salick at the time acknowledges a beautiful young blonde who he tried to set up with one of the boys.

Our camp was now in Coralici and I remember us driving out to Bihac to help rebuild and paint a hospital. We were now on our second tour in Drvar (Bosnia), and I remember the Italians coming to our camp. We were all training together for riot control. The reason for this, the Muslims were planning to reopen their mosques and they anticipated problems from the Croatians. We were now in position in Mostar, all the boys were ready for action however the Croatians became wise, they looked at us, they did not engage us. We were on standby for a second mosque however it was called off as everything was peaceful.

Tango with Death

It was a very interesting month thus far. An electrical engineer, who had gone up on a rooftop to connect some wires, was electrocuted by a fluke lightening flash. Two weeks later a Cougar armoured vehicle travelling to Zgon from our camp rolled over and killed the driver while injuring two other soldiers. My night patrol (2300-0700 hours) was now ready to go out into a new area, with very narrow roads, and heavily wooded valley. The patrol was going rather smoothly, and suddenly, around 0200 hours, my front right wheel started to give way as though a landslide was occurring. I pulled to the left, but it was too late as my seat pin was unhooked and I was now at the pit of the driver's compartment, slamming my lower back/tailbone. I felt as though my private parts were pushed into my stomach. The rolling continued, and I was now moving towards the hatch. I saw the hatch cover coming down towards my head, I attempted with a soccer move to head-butt the hatch cover to cushion the impact. When the vehicle stopped rolling, the hatch cover had pinned my neck. I heard Bohrsons' voice. I then said to Bohrson, "come and take this crap off my neck." My legs were numb and my arms were basically paralyzed. I knew all the boys were banged up, but they continued as if the crash had never happened because they had a mission to complete. I remember Sgt. Wayne Evans (John Wayne of this era), very calm and collective, saying to the boys check each other for injuries and account for the kit.

Ben Brown continues

I remember the Croatians tried to take over the town Martinbrod. They blew up the bridge that allowed people easy access to their township which made life difficult to get to the center (hospital, restaurants, shopping). They would be forced to walk 5 kilometers to get to the center. After the war it was very difficult, furthermore we were there to provide security for these people, day and night.

I remember our patrol going to the old train station by the head of the tunnel where you could not enter the tunnel because it was full of mines.

FROM HOSTILITY TO PEACE THROUGH FOOTBALL

One evening while patrolling Velika Kladusa at approximately 23:30 hours there was a group of young men making noise on a tennis court, I directed our combat drive to the tennis court. As we got closer to the courts, they became hostile and very vociferous, "SFOR Go home, SFOR Go home." We arrived at the court, "boys cover me," I dismounted the vehicle and said to the interpreter, "Elvis lets go." I approached the few hostile young people and I observed two older gentlemen and I greeted them "dobra vecer" (good evening in Serbian-Croatian), and I asked, "what is the problem?" and one of the older men stated, this Albanian refugee wants to play football with us and most of us do not want them in our country, much less to play football with us, Bosnia is for Bosnians, not for Serb's, Croats, refugees and not for SFOR to run our country. I stated that's a long list of problems, therefore let's discuss them one by one, we are here to help you to keep the Serbs and Croats out, so you can rebuild your country,

We are not here to run your country, we are trying to keep things peaceful, the noise that you are making are keeping some of your country men and women awake and some are scared. To solve this problem, pick your best 5 players and we will play a game. The young ones and one of the mature gentleman stated, "Canadians cannot play football," I said no problem, I walked towards the vehicle, took my jacket and pistol off, and I said to my boys "look at this." Myself, the Albanian kid and three Bosnians that the rest thought were terrible players became a team. I called Elvis to explain to the three Bosnians, tonight you want to show your super star friends you are better than them, you must play hard and stay very close to three players on the opposing team and when the ball is passed to them kick it away or pass to myself or the Albanian youngster.

I looked at the Albanian kid, "do you understand German," he said 'a little', I said "that is good," I ask him, "can you dance with the ball?" "Yes" we communicated through German words, this young Albanian kid was very talented, he played hard and he had speed, I did my job of a defensive mid field to neutralize their attack and distribute the ball on our attack to my fellow players. On other occasions I will take the ball up the middle on the attack, one of my soldiers "stated shots fired," the game ended. We played for 30 minutes, no one scored, the two mature men at the end, embrace me and said "Havala" (thank you in Serbian-Croatian). they continued to state, "next time bring some more Canadians to play," and I replied, "thank you and do not discriminate, we need people to help us rebuild your country and I would like to come and live here after my military service." He asks 'really?' I said, "yes you are the most wonderful people I have met in my life, I would like to come here and work for you, you must promise me you will let me play football with all of you, good evening, until we meet again."

2001

Another vehicle patrol and another situation to entertain. While on patrol, an older Croatian gentleman who we brought back to his home the day before as he was a displaced refugee as a result of the war. He flagged our vehicle down and mentioned that there is a fowl scent in the air. It was maybe about 800 meters away. I decided to dismount my boys leaving the driver Ben Brown and the machine gunner on the vehicle. Approaching closer, the stench was unbearable. I thought this may be a couple of dead animals, or maybe one or two people had a shootout and their bodies had been left there.

Approaching the site, many people had been buried in the same site, I turned towards the signaler who contacted headquarters to inform them of what was going on. We set up a perimeter around the site; within 20 minutes the professionals came in their white coveralls, spraying and digging. The findings of the professionals relayed to us that 98 people of the same village were buried in the same hole; men, women, and children. We mounted our vehicle and we went to the village to do an area sweep. Upon reaching the village, we dismounted and searched every household, every barn, every building, and there was no sight of life to be found, it was a ghost village. To imagine, here is a village where people live, where they smile, they have functions, and because of ethnic hatred, the result is a horrific massacre.

It was the Spring of 2001, the Muslims in Bana Luka wanted to restore their mosque however Croatians opposed the idea, hence SFOR presence was needed. We were debriefed on our task and what we will be doing. While patrolling through a square walking with my boys towards the mosque, a voice with a strong British accent amidst the crowd "hey black man," he appeared in front of me, "look at what America did to you people and you are willing to die for them." I stated "we are Canadians, I am not here to discuss yesterday, we are here, to ensure that the Muslims could restore their mosque and furthermore, if you promise me you will have peace in this country by this evening, me and boys will be the first to go back to Canada." He looked at me, and my boys, and stated, "at least you are not the gunslingers of America."

One of the most remarkable events that will happen on our patrols when seeking out information to provide assistance in safeguarding or making life better for the local people was their kindness that they displayed. They had very little yet they would offer us Turkish coffee, sometimes food, that in itself, was displaying a remarkable human kindness and sometimes they would acknowledge our boys that have been on the road for at least fourteen hours providing security for them.

The following is from a Canadian Magazine: Maple Leaf 2001.

DRVAR, Bosnia-Herzegovina — MCpl Derek Salick, of Oscar Company, 3 RCR Battle Group, poses with the Milne family, who returned in April from Belgrade, Yugoslavia, to their home in the village of Martin Brod. The 73-year-old father told MCpl Salick that his village still lacked telephones, some homes were without electricity and 400 families have yet to return home to the area. He also said that some of the village children were homeless and there weren't enough seeds for the vegetable gardens.

MCpl Salick, a 19-year CF veteran, knows he's helping to maintain a safe and secure environment for the Bosnian people. "When I hear your patrol vehicles at night, I sleep in peace," one villager told him. Serving on his second tour in Bosnia, MCpl Salick wants to do more on a personal level to help the people he meets while patrolling. He has started a newsletter for his family and friends in Canada and in Trinidad and Tobago. The newsletter's aim is to inform readers about what he sees in Bosnia and ask for useful items—from seeds to warm clothing. To receive MCpl Salick's newsletter, contact him at abdullahsalick@hotmail.com

www.forces.gc.ca/site/community/mapleleaf

It was July 2001, in Drvar, Bosnia. Imagine a beautiful soccer field and an empty stadium, with many young people around it, afraid to do anything. After asking several questions, as patrol commander, on the status of the field, I was told that during the war, many anti-personnel mines were scattered all over the field. Several local youths lost their legs, arms, and some even their lives, because the mines were disguised as toys for children. The children would attempt to kick a ball, but instead lose their leg, or pick a toy, and as a result would lose an arm. We sent a report through and up the chain of command, and they acted on the report, via sending Canadian combat engineers to assess the field and clear the field of all anti-personnel mines and land mines.

A game was then organized between the Dutch contingent soccer team, and our rifle Company(Oscar) soccer team. All local government officials were present, our Commanding Officer (CO) and Regimental Sergeant Major (RSM) was also present. Never before was the stadium packed with locals, and around the field were the same young people; some were shirtless even, but they were there to witness this event. Many of the locals came to support the Canadians because we had been present advocates for their community and they knew this. The air was alive. The game commenced at 18:00 hours. The Dutch had first touch; they were knocking the ball, short passes, medium and long passes. Our team started off very defensive; we didn't believe in losing, ensuring they didn't get into our eighteen-yard box. On our team we had, Ivan Karin, a Croatian-Canadian, Plocica and Binczack, our Polish brothers, Briand, he was Jewish, and myself, of Trinidadian background, however we were all Canadians willing to stand in defense of our international policies with our lives.

The Dutch were the first to score off a corner kick. At the end of the first half, the score was 1-0. During the break, we realized the formation to attack. Three-two-five; three defenders, two mid-fielders and five forwards to attack. As the second half commenced, from the touch we maintain possession of the ball in their half of the field. After fifteen minutes, we had scored our second goal, and we reverted to a four-four-two formation. The Dutch went into a four-three-three formation, and they were now using their wing-backs as attackers. Near the end of the game the Dutch scored their second goal. Tied, we went into overtime. The ref called, "Next goal wins!" The Dutch had the first touch of the ball.

Our Canadian soldier's mentality was to go for the victory, and give everything, so we attacked. As the last stopper, even I went into their side of the field. They had a speedy center forward, Robert, and his two inside forwards, both on me. I jockeyed and then tackled for the ball, he passed it to the right of me, as we made contact we were now both on the ground and his mate scored the goal as it was now two players on the goalie. The Dutch won the game 3-2. At game's end, our Commanding Officer (CO) and Regimental Sergeant Major (RSM) came down to congratulate us on our efforts. Simultaneously, the dignitaries applauded all the players, and at the sight of this, the young people regained their confidence to go back on that field. Although we lost the game, our mission was accomplished; those young people could finally use that field again. Thereafter my platoon commander received a message that our platoon has been tasked to Macedonia to participate in Operation Harvest.

MACEDONIA 2001

In 2001, Macedonia the only peacefully separated formerly Yugoslavian Republic, was in escalated crisis of insurgency and aggressive attacks by the National Liberation Army (NLA) against the Republic of Macedonia. In short, the goal and purpose of the NLA-who were of Albanian ethnicity-was a greater Albania. I will debate that assumption because while on the ground in Skopje Macedonia I conversed with quite a few young Albanian Macedonians, they stated that after Tito's death, the Macedonian government was slowly removing their language from the education system and slowly suppressing their culture. Hence, from this action, came the conflict with arms. The hostilities continued and reached alarming global concerns, when Macedonian security forces responded (sure they will win) with force threatening another civil war or another Kosovo. NATO Secretary General Lord Robertson, at the time, stated that for: "a country that was functioning good, which managed to avoid the great horror of Bosnia, Kosovo, Serbia, Krajina, Eastern Slovenia and to get into a civil war, now, it would be a great tragedy" (Macedonian/Albanian language daily, Friday 29th June, 2001).

The conflict between the security forces of the Republic of Macedonia and the National Liberation Army (Ethnic Albanians) began February

2001 and ended with the OHRID Agreement. By August 2001, 170,000 people were displaced, majority were Macedonians.

> *"Operation "Essential Harvest"[drawn up in response to a request for NATO assistance made by President Trajkovski on the 20th of June] was officially launched on 22 August and effectively started on 27 August. This 30-day mission involved the sending of approximately 3500 NATO troops, with logistical support, to disarm ethnic Albanian groups and destroy their weapons"* (SFOR Informer#121, September 5, 2001).

The United Nations sanctioned the intervention which was enacted by NATO forces. The UN/NATO forces waded into the conflict in the hopes of ceasing the violence, so that civilized society could begin to function again. This was the right intention to bring hope to a hopeless situation. Further, this intervention had every chance of success. The combined military might of the NATO forces was fully capable of engaging the warring factions in Macedonia, using the force necessary to ensure the cessation of hostilities, demilitarization and disarming the NLA. Furthermore, NATO Secretary General Lord Robertson pointed out that "NATO mission in Macedonia will not be Pro-Albanian nor Pro-Macedonian" (Macedonian/Albanian language daily, June, 2001). The objective of the mission, was a successful outcome of political dialogue between different parties in former Yugoslavian Republic of Macedonia, towards an agreement to peace plan providing for the introduction of confidence-building measures and the "cessation of hostilities as an essential precondition for any NATO assistance" (Statement by the North Atlantic Council June 20, 2001).

OPERATION FORAGE –SEPTEMBER 2001
FORMER YUGOSLAVIA REPUBLIC OF MACEDONIA

Master Corporal Derek (Slick) Salick of the 3rd Battalion. The Royal Canadian Regiment stands gate guard in the Canadian contingent in the NATO mission:

OPERATION ESSENTIAL HARVEST - NATO.

The mission deployed troops to disarm insurgents after a cease fire agreement.

The following is a statement by NATO Secretary General, Lord Robertson following the North Atlantic Council decision to launch Operation Essential Harvest:

> *"Today (Aug. 22) is an important day for NATO and an even more important one for the former Yugoslav Republic of Macedonia (FYROM). Today we are taking an historic step forward for wider stability and security in the Balkans. At 12 noon, the North Atlantic Council decided to authorize SACEUR to issue the Activation Order for Operation Essential Harvest. At that time, however, we agreed a set of four pre-conditions would have to be met for the 30-day deployment to take place: - a political agreement signed by the main Parliamentary Leaders; - a status of forces agreement (SOFA) with FYROM (Former Yugoslavia Republic of Macedonia) and agreed conditions for the Task Force; - an agreed plan for weapons collection, including an explicit agreement by the ethnic Albanian armed groups to disarm; and- an enduring cease-fire. This initiative was endorsed by the political leaders of FYROM. The result is that today the North Atlantic Council has given authority to SACEUR to deploy Task Force Harvest and to start collecting and destroying the weapons of the ethnic Albanian insurgents. The decision made today by the NAC was a very positive one. The legitimate democratic representatives of the people of the former Yugoslav Republic of Macedonia can count on NATO's commitment to assist them on the road to peace and stability"* (SFOR Informer#121, September 5, 2001).

Expressing all our feelings, Capt. Guy Turpin states that: "It was with great surprise and enthusiasm that the 3rd Royal Canadian Regiment Battle Group received a warning order Tuesday, Aug. 21. They have to assist in the 30-day mission to disarm the National Liberation Army's forces in the Former Yugoslav Republic of Macedonia (FYROM), under the auspices of Operation Essential Harvest" (SFOR Informer#121, September 5, 2001). From the beginning, I understood our mission as very important, having experienced the human drama, pain and violence in Kosovo and Bosnia. The importance of the mission depended on the swift disarmament of the radical fighters of NLA (National Liberation Army) and a commitment to a political dialogue towards peaceful negotiations on the road to peace, reconciliation, and stability.

The above photo is the arrival of Canadian Tank/Infantry soldiers arriving in Macedonia. Our job will be to collect weapons and destroy them, provide security, continuous patrols, and setting up Observation Points (OPs). I remember one of the patrols where young men would turn their weapons in. I assume that they were too young to understand what they were fighting for. They were clearly manipulated by older men to pick up arms so that they, the older men, would be richer at the end of the day. At that moment, my mind ran on Soulliere, as he remembered the line from the movie, Rambo: "War-old men start it, young men fight it, nobody wins and everyone in the middle dies." I could further argue that many people suffer, especially women and children who are raped and abused. They often suffer from PTSD that so many people tend to forget. It is as though women do not matter in the equation of life.

Another sad day, we just got back from a ten-hour patrol and within two hours we were all assembled under a tent and CNN was presenting the 9/11 attack over and over. We, the soldiers, were now on red-alert; expect anything, be aware more than before. This attack was shown to us over and over, not for us to have fear, however to be ready at all times. At that moment, I was pretty upset. Here we are, trying to make the world a better place for humanity, and the ignorant bastards have decided to attack my home. I felt helpless because I can't defend my own.

Chapter 4: Rape as Psychological Warfare

WOMEN OF THE WORLD

Oh women of the world,
Oppression has no bounds,
For you, 'cause it is colorless,
You are a gift from above.
Our forefathers did not know how to appreciate thee,
Therefore, they placed you behind them.

Oh women of the world,
Take your stand beside me.
The lessons of our forefathers,
Have enabled us to disrespect and ignore your strength.

Oh women of the world,
Take your stand beside me.
You have shown us strength,
You have always given us hope,
For a brighter 'morrow,
Without you there will be a world of emptiness.

Oh women of the world,
Take your stand beside me,
For in the morning, we would like you to
Teach the children about rights and wrongs,
What you once taught us.
We plead with thee to forever guide and strengthen our society
With your great knowledge and understanding.

Oh women of the world,
Take your stand beside me.
Let us move forward with greater strides together,
Standing united, forever strong,
For a brighter morrow.
Therefore, take your stand,
Women of the world.

Salick

> "Emphasis was placed on women's responsibility for the cultural and biological reproduction of the newly forming nation-states;" which resulted "in the proliferation of public policies that were aimed at controlling women's reproductive sphere" (Zadruga)

> "Gendered violence in war draws on peacetime meanings of sexuality. In peacetime, even as we near the end of the 20th century, control of women by men and protection of their sexuality continue to be convenient means of justifying the domination of women by men in southeastern Europe." (Maria Olujic, 1990)

> "The dynamic of male protection of female honor is embedded in the complex traditional cultures of the Slavic peoples in southeastern Europe. Here, the center of the patriarchal regime is the extended family, called zadruga, a corporate family unit under which all holdings—for example, property, livestock, and land—are held communally by the patrilineage (Byrnes 1976; Hammel 1968, 1972; Tomasevich 1976). Zadruga ideology has persisted for centuries and is the crux of Yugoslavian cultural ideologies." (Maria Olujic, 1990)

It was a beautiful cold morning and I was asked to take a foot patrol into Velika Kladusa. I decided to switch up my route; I took some back roads, landmines free. While on the route we heard a song banging on the rooftops. I went forward to the house where the noise was coming from. As I entered the yard, I noticed plum trees on my right and left; plums littered the ground.

I am now knocking on the door, and I am saying 'dobra dan' (meaning good day). An older lady opened the top half of the door and replied, "dobra dan." With the help of my patrol interpreter, we started a conversation with the woman. She offered us Turkish coffee. I turned to my boys and asked them, "do you want some coffee?" They replied, "no, not now." Being kind I decided to say, thank you, "hvala." She invited myself and my interpreter in. As we entered, there were four young girls each wearing black clothing with their hijabs. I attempted to greet them warmly by saying, "dobra dan." The girls were reluctant to reply and maintained a serious/stern look in their faces. They were present but only as seemingly empty shells, lacking emotion.

As a good soldier I looked around, I noticed plums in jars, plum juice, and plums on a large and old wooden table. The older lady began to make coffee; she suddenly came over to us. She asked, "Are you the Canadian solider that goes to the mosque on Fridays?" I replied, "Yes."

She then looked at me, shook her head, and asked, "Where are you from?" She began to rub the top of my hand as though she were expecting the color of my hand to change; it was strange I thought. She then repeated the question again, "Where are you from?" I said, "Canada." She shook her head, no. I looked at Elvis, my interpreter, he asked, "Where were you born?" I then replied, "I was born in Trinidad but lived my life in Canada." She stopped rubbing my hand and said, "Ok." Thereafter one of the young girls gave me a Turkish coffee and I turned to her and said havala/thank you.

The woman suddenly walked over to a rocking chair made of old wicker and said, "This is where they tied my hands and legs to the chair; they had a gun to my head while they repeatedly raped my four grand daughter who were 8, 9, 10 and 11 years old." To add further insult to injury these men humiliated these young girls by urinating on them. "My young girls are shamed within the community," she said. I realised that the Islamic religion and Eastern European culture viewed them as worthless in the community due to the loss of their virginity and strong influence of the patriarchy in place. I was not expecting such a horrific story. I was hesitant to look at the young girls being a man myself after having heard of the trauma inflicted upon them.

I turned, I looked back to see pain in their faces along with tears welling up in their eyes. And to deflect myself from looking at them, the grandmother carried on, "My husband, two sons, and their mother were killed during the war." I then looked at Elvis, I asked, "Is this for real?" He replied, "Yes, people do not want them here." I said to her, "My heart hurts. I will make a report. How can we help you from now on?" She replied, "No one can help us." I observed only plums, I suspected they were lacking any real food. I then told the woman, "We Canadians can assist you with humanitarian aid and ensure you are safe in your home." At that time SFOR did not have any programs in place for these situations.

I then went outside the flat, I asked my boys, "Do any one of you want to leave your box lunch? I will buy you lunch in VK city centre." They all gave me their box lunches, I proceeded to give it to the woman and her four young granddaughters. I said to her, "Thank you for your kindness. Thank you for sharing your story. I would like you to go to the Canadian base, they will likely help you." I then left the premises and went to the home of the older gentleman, who continuously pester them.

> *"Women marry into their husband's families and are thus outside of the core social unit. They are valued as sex objects, mothers,*

and workers (Denich 1974; Stein Erlich 1966). This pattern is familiar to much of the Mediterranean: women represent the code of honor of the family and the code of shame via the blood revenge for non-family member's transgressions, which along with a male-dominated strict hierarchy, provide many behavioral norms and unity (Boehm 1984; Davis 1977; Simic 1983; Woodward 1985)." (Olujic 1990).

"The honor/shame dichotomy is evident in the highly guarded aspects of women's virginity, chastity, marital virtue, and especially fertility. For women, honor and shame are the basis of morality and underpin the three-tiered hierarchy of statuses: husband, family, and village. In the former Yugoslavia, these traditional values regarding sexual behavior, which condoned rape through honor/ shame constraints, took precedence over economic transformations, state policy commitments under communism, and male migration." (Olujic 1990).

"One night in September, a group of Bosnian Serbs took a group of women and their children from the nearby Partizan Sports Hall to a nearby apartment building; three of them were Sanela, Fikreta, and Nusreta...Fikreta's four-year-old daughter was also taken with her. She was able to watch through an open door as her mother was stripped, searched for valuables and, as a pistol was put to her head, was then raped by four men. "They told me they would like us to give birth to Cetnik children...They told me 'we will do everything so that you never even think of returning', the woman reported" (Amnesty International Document, 1997: 4).

"Whether a woman is raped by soldiers in her home or is held in a house with other women and raped over and over again, she is raped with a political purpose – to intimidate, humiliate, and degrade her and others affected by her suffering. The effect of rape is often to ensure that women and their families will flee and never return" (Stigimayer, 1994: P.85).

This use of unrestrained force, unchecked by any notion of morality or civil society, became the Status Quo for the conflict. As Alexandra Stigimayer (1994), states in her book Mass Rape: The War Against Women in Bosnia-Herzegovina: "...to varying degrees, all parties have violated humanitarian law, or the laws of war. Bosnians, Croatians, and Serbians, the only difference is that the latter did it on a larger scale" (Stigimayer, 1994:10).

Mass rape was used as a tool, a weapon, a method of clearing out an area, just as much as the other means used to enact ethnic cleansing and the mass murder of civilians.

Rape in the Bosnian war, pertains to the characteristic elements of "War Rape" in the ethnic clash between Serbs, Croats, and Bosnians. While on a lesser scale, women of all ethnic groups were affected, more specifically, rape was used as a systematized instrument of war by the Bosnian Serb forces of the Army of the Republika Srpska (VRS), predominantly targeting women and girls of the Bosnian ethnic group for physical and moral destruction (Snyder et al 2006 pg.189-90). The figures are stunning. Estimates of the total number of women raped during the war range from 25,000 to 50,000 (Ibid). This has been referred to as "mass rape" particularly with regard to the coordinated use of rape as a weapon of war. Although the raping of women was used as a weapon of war, this only demonstrates how barbaric men are. Now these wounds were permanent, hence the reason war never finishes.

Historically men as citizens of the state were emphasized, while women were placed in the same position as slaves. This ideology of inequality still exists and continues to drive the motives of men in the present. As we did our patrols, and came upon these women, we saw that their souls had been stolen. The hopelessness, the futile expressions on their face, brought sadness to my boys and me. We found that Canadian soldiers, as account of the influence from the nation they were proudly brought up in, respected women far more than most. It was an honour walking with men who would do anything for their country, while risking their lives to ensure that the peace they knew at home could reach these women.

We see new cultures, entering Canada, and they deny women their basic rights, unfortunately, we allow these indignities to happen. I believe that when these new cultures come to Canada, they must be educated in the proper treatment of women, in order to learn to respect and give women their equal space. The aforementioned is what our nation needs to improve in order to place ourselves in a position where we can properly teach and be an example for women's rights Globally. While conversing with these women, their conversation was simple, continually saying, "I'm only waiting for death." They had lost everything and that they could hope for. They once had dreams, ambitions, and family, this was all taken from them, in addition to the mental and physical abuse. They were shells of themselves; almost zombie like. You could see the pain in their eyes and hear it in their voice. Furthermore, these were Islamic communities, where the Muslim men prided themselves in marrying a virgin. These women who had been raped, had lost their place in their community; the belief is women were supposed to be married. The only hope these women had was to leave the country and start life all over, and that option was a very difficult one to achieve.

Many of these atrocities stemmed from spontaneous actions from individuals and groups as well as from a coherent policy of what I choose to call physical as well as 'psychological genocide'. Indeed, studies have shown that the forms of terror inflicted on the populace in the region all had a random as well as rational temper. In other words, "rape" is seen here as a "weapon of war." According to the First Interim Report 1992 (S/25274), of the United Nations Commission on Breaches of Geneva law in Former Yugoslavia.

Some of the reported rape and sexual assault cases committed by Serbs, mostly against Muslims, are clearly the result of individual or small group conduct without evidence of command direction or an overall policy. However, many more seem to be a part of an overall pattern whose characteristics include: similarities among practices in non-contiguous geographic areas, simultaneous commission of other international humanitarian law violations, simultaneous military activity, simultaneous activity to displace civilian populations, common elements in the commission of rape, maximizing shame and humiliation to not only the victim, but also the victim's community. One factor in particular that leads to this conclusion is the timing of the rapes. A large number of rapes which occurred in places of detention did not appear to be random. Hence they indicate at least a policy of encouraging rape supported by the deliberate failure of camp commanders and local authorities to exercise command and control over the personnel under their authority (Ibid).

Other reports stated that the perpetrators said they were ordered to rape. While others said that the aim was to ensure the victims and their families would never return to the area. Perpetrators told the female victims that they would bear children of the perpetrator's ethnicity. That they would become pregnant and then be held in custody until it was too late to get an abortion. In other cases, victims were threatened that if they told anyone they would be hunted down and killed (Ibid).

Numerous rape camps were set up across the Serb controlled town of Foca. To date, "Karaman House" has remained a particularly well-studied case in judicial terms. There, Muslim females, including minors as young as 12, were repeatedly raped. In the findings of the related Kunarac trial, the appalling conditions of the detention centers being used for mass rape were described (Ibid). Women were kept in various detention centers where they had to live in intolerably unhygienic conditions. They were mistreated in many ways including, for many of them, being raped repeatedly. Serb soldiers or policemen would come to these detention centers, select one or more women, take them out and rape them. All this was done in full view, in complete knowledge and sometimes with the direct involvement of the local authorities, particularly the police forces. The head of Foca police forces, Dragan Gagović, was personally identified as one of the men who came to these detention centers to take women out and rape them repeatedly (International Criminal Tribunal for the Former Yugoslavia, Kunaractrial, Findings of the trial chamber).

The Serbians will say, "If we cannot kill them, we'll breed it out of them." "For the Serbs, the desire to degrade, humiliate and impregnate Bosnian Muslim women with 'little Chetniks' was paramount" (Ibid). Women were forced to go full term with their pregnancies and give birth. In other reports, the methods used to inflict pain and humiliation on the female ethnic population, were of surreal dimensions. At the height of the conflict in the former Yugoslavia, one incident stands out where the women knew the rapes would begin when 'Marsna Drinu' was played over the loudspeaker of the main mosque. 'Marsna Drinu,' or 'March on the Drina', is reportedly a former Chetnik fighting song that was banned during the Tito years. While 'Marsna Drinu' was playing, the women were ordered to strip and soldiers entered the homes taking the ones they wanted. The age of women taken ranged from 12 to 60. Frequently the soldiers would seek out mother and daughter combinations, and many women were severely beaten during the rapes (Seventh Report on War Crimes in the Former Yugoslavia: Part II US submission of information to the United Nations Security Council).

As far as the psychological and physical effects of rape, in a study of 68 Croatian and Bosniak victims of rape during the 1992-1995 war found that many suffered psychological problems as a result. None had any psychiatric history prior to the rapes. After the rapes, 25 of them had suicidal thoughts, 58 suffered from depression immediately after, and 52 were still suffering from depression one year later. Of the women, 44 had been raped more than once and 21 of them had been raped daily throughout their captivity. Twenty-nine of them had become pregnant and 17 had abortions. The study reached the conclusion that the rapes had "deep immediate and long-term consequences on the mental-health" of the women (Ibid).

Following the end of hostilities in the region, which ended with the U.S. engineered 1995 Dayton Agreement, much attention has been paid to the need to understand the reality of what happened, dispel myths, and for responsible leaders to be brought to justice and be encouraged to accept their guilt for the mass rapes and other atrocities. Historians such as Niall Ferguson assessed a key factor behind the high-level decision to use mass rape for ethnic cleansing as being misguided nationalism.

Prior to 1980, Croatian and Serbian nationalism had been effectively repressed by Marshal Tito which did nothing to diminish the intensity of nationalist longings. Slobodan Milosevic took the opportunity to inflame the Serbian populace by invoking the mythology of 'victimhood' which called for taking a more aggressive stance towards Bosniaks. Feelings of victimhood and aggression towards Bosniaks were further stirred up with exaggerated tales about the role played by a small fraction of Bosnian Muslims in the Ustase genocide of Serbs in the 1940s. Other myths invoked included suggestions that Bosnian Muslims were racially different, typically that they were actually of largely Turkish blood, when, in fact, DNA tests have shown that both groups appear to share the same gene pool typical of South Slavs (Ibid). Nevertheless, government-led hate campaigns against Muslims became the norm; including instances whereby government troops would announce by loud speaker that "every Serb who protects a Muslim will be killed immediately" (Ibid).

In the aftermath of the conflict, ethnic identity is now of much greater social importance in Bosnia than it was prior to 1992. From the 1960s to the war, the percentage of mixed marriages between communities has been close to 12% and young citizens would often refer to themselves as Bosnians rather than identifying their ethnicity. After the conflict, it had become mandatory to be identified as either Bosniak or Serb or Croat, and this has been a problem for the children of rape victims as they come of age (Ibid).

MUJIN

On my patrols, the local people I encountered related to me in a very trusting manner. I believe that some saw me as a friendly face because we prayed in the same mosque. As my foot patrols continued, I met a young boy named Mujin. He was 10 years old and he knew a great deal about downtown Velika Kladusa: every side road, every short cut and, more importantly, he knew where most of the anti-personnel mines were located. What a brilliant young man I thought! He was not the only one though. I met a lot of these impoverished young children, boys and girls. Their parents had died in the war, or should I say, during the destruction of Bosnia.

This particular city had a population of 50,000 people before the war. However, in 1998 the population was down to 7,500 people. It was now made up of Bosnians, Albanian refugees, gypsies and many homeless children. Mujin was a little more fortunate than the others. He lived in a partially destroyed home with his 80-year-old grandmother. Mujin knew most of the other youngsters. His best friend was Tanija, a little angel of a girl who was his neighbor. He was intensely interested in becoming a footballer. He would say to me, "Salick, I am 10 years old. I pay 2 deutsche marks/month to train for football. A few years from now, I will score many goals and make millions and I will rebuild my country." Tanija too, had her own dreams. She wanted to be a kick boxer and learn to shoot weapons to protect her grandmother. I wanted them all to be successful in life and felt that the SFOR mission could create space and opportunity for these young people. In fact, during these moments, when they shared their dreams and aspirations, I really felt that we had a common purpose. I would bask in the high energy they displayed and truly believed that they represented a great hope and a bright future for their country. Their infectious laughter and ready smiles was what I looked forward to on my patrols.

One Saturday morning our section was on Quick Reaction Force (QRF), and from higher command we were dispatched to capture the war criminal in our Area of Responsibility (AOR). After five hours of cat and mouse they were assisted by their Croatian comrades, they crossed the border into Croatia and escaped. We discussed what we were going to do next and decided to take our Armored Vehicle General Purpose (AVGP) to make up for lost time: but is time actually ever 'lost'? I remember well, at the time that our Area of Responsibility (AOR) was huge; so I decided to do my patrol route in a reverse fashion. This time, I told myself, I would begin my patrol on the outskirts of the city before going in. By the time we entered the city, it was midday. As soon as we got there, I was told that Mujin, my young friend, was looking for me. Since my boys were hungry, and I did not know how urgent things were, we ate before we made our way towards Mujin's Grandmother's house.

As soon as Mujin heard the sound of the approaching vehicle, he came running out of Tanija's Grandmother's house. Grabbing my hand, he briskly marched me to Tanija's door where I learnt, through an interpreter, that Tanija was raped by two men. As she laid on the floor, still and silent, I felt immensely helpless. My body trembled with anger. I was angry with myself because I felt that I had failed this young girl. I couldn't stand being in there any longer and went outside. As I stepped out the door, my body felt a cold inner draft. I shivered. I wanted to cry, but I could not. I am a soldier, I said to myself, I am a rock; signs of weakness will not be displayed by this soldier, not today. Yet, this was not the kind of pain I was used to. I could not take a pain killer and make the pain disappear. It was an inward pain. As these thoughts were running through my mind, Tanijas' Grandmother came outside and held my hand for a moment, and said," It's okay." But I knew then that the image of this broken young girl would be engraved in my mind until my death

THEORIES OF WARTIME RAPE

Biology based theories for understanding wartime rape hold that rape is something "natural" to men, a biologically determined behavior (Snyder et al., 2006:185). Thus rape that occurs during wartime is not distinct to the war rather a natural occurrence regardless of the situation—time period, geographical space or social conditions for example, it is something distinct to men. What is distinct about wartime situations are the environments of chaos in which men's natural sexual aggression is released via the "spoils of war"—women's bodies (Ibid). In this understanding rape is understood as an inevitable outcome of war. The author will argue that this theory is lacking as it does not give an explanation for or acknowledge men who do not rape, furthermore I will also state 'men in their barbaric state would commit such beastly crimes against women', calling the biological determinant of this theory into question (Ibid:186). Historically this understanding of rape during war has resulted in the normalization of rape in such circumstances, as such, "raped women have traditionally remained socially invisible... (Ibid).

Feminist theories on wartime rape differ from biology based theories in that it holds gender to be an important factor in relation to the silencing of its occurrence publicly, where biology based theories have ignored this connection. Understanding what took place during the Bosnian conflict from a feminist perspective would suggest that rape occurred as a result of socialization. It is patriarchal cultures which socialize men, "to despise women, often on an unconscious level, and rape in times of war offers them an opportunity to vent their contempt for women" (Ibid). The authors go on to note, "rape and sexual torture in war are seen as being motivated by a man's desire to dominate and oppress women," in a classical feminist position (Ibid:187).

Gender relations in the Former Yugoslavia: a look into the history of gender relations within Yugoslavia prior to its breakup revels a society very much dominated by patriarchal rule and dominance as well as extended family closeness. Once married, a woman would move into her husband's famillal house where she would then come under the authority of her husband's parents (Ibid). Additionally, women would come to represent and symbolize patriarchal familial (Zadruga) honour/shame, and as a result much attention was given to their "chastity, marital virtue, and fertility," creating a situation of Yugoslav identity very much so concerned with this zadruga ideology (Ibid). Yugoslavia was in a unique position compared to other Communist Bloc countries in that it was generally connected to and exposed to the outside world, with foreign literature, communication, and ideas entering. Yugoslavia's connection to the outside world was noticeable in its women's movement which occurred in the late 1970s. By 1979, "a women's movement was officially in place with the formation of the Women and Society in Zagreb, a feminist organization that fanned out across Yugoslavia" (Ibid: 188). However, despite this in the 1980s Yugoslavia's feminist movement would come into conflict with another movement throughout the Federation—Nationalism with communism on its way out following the death of Tito in 1980 (Ibid).

As the Yugoslavian Federation was collapsing and ethnic nationalism continued to rise, both Serbian and Croatian leadership envisioned the expansion of Serbia and Croatia which would include the land that would later become Bosnia, when Bosnia declared independence in 1992, with Serbian leadership seeking 62% of the territory and Croatia seeking to create a territory from the remaining land (Ibid, 189). Subsequently, "When Bosnia declared its independence from Yugoslavia in 1992, Serb nationalist launched a war that produced a campaign of killing, mayhem, and mass rape" (Ibid).

The number of women who were raped during the Bosnian conflict is something that cannot accurately be determined as non-disclosure of such of such events is encouraged under the gender dynamics in the region and Zadruga ideology, where not identifying as being raped offered a way to escape the social stigma to the woman and her family. Estimates point to between 25,000-50,000 women being raped during the Bosnian conflict, with the vast majority of rapes executed by Serbs attacking Muslim women (Ibid). This can be attributed to the Serbs possessing a greater military force than the other factions in the conflict as well as the Serb adoption of rape as a strategy for achieving ethnic cleansing (Ibid:189-90).

The authors highlight that the, "overall tactic of war rape was to humiliate, stigmatize, and terrorize women so completely that Muslims would leave the territory and never return" (Ibid)Snyder et al., 2006, p.190). Additionally, "war rape would not work as well as a policy of terror were it not for the cultural salience within the honor/shame complex generalized in the southeastern European cultural area" (Ibid).

The authors' attention to a range of dynamics which occurred in the region prior to the outbreak of the Bosnian war speaks to their position that it was much more than the situation of war that attributed to wartime rape, as biology based theories on rape would suggest. Coming from a feminist perspective the authors give attention to the recent history of Bosnia to explain how the incident of wartime rape came about. Specifically contributing factors to the happening of wartime rape during the Bosnian war guided by the Snyder et al. included the gender relations in the former Yugoslavia, as well as the rise of nationalism, giving a complex understanding of abuse against women which occurred during the Bosnian war.

International intervention in Bosnia was based on "principles of territoriality rather than on humanitarian concern" (Rodgers, 2001:183). Rodgers holds that there has been a pattern of international intervention in conflict since the Cold War of territoriality—"traditional principles of state sovereignty and inter-state conflict," over humanitarian concern (Ibid). This meaning that it is territoriality which motivates international actors to become involved in conflict and not humanitarian concern, irrespective of the agenda which is publicly promoted.

According to Rodgers (2001), international intervention in the Bosnia conflict was fundamentally flawed. This was on account of several factors which generally tended to ignore the situation of women; with the author holding that human rights abuses which were occurring against women were ignored by the international community and thus, not a factor for intervention. It was not, "human rights abuse, and in particular crimes of sexual violence against women, [which were] subsumed to be a 'state-strategist' agenda," rather principles of state sovereignty which prompted international intervention (Ibid: 183). As such, Rodgers indicates, "that there is a fundamental feminist dilemma at the heart of debates on the ethics of intervention," holding acceptance of a feminist agenda is inherent with difficulties in, "male-dominated, masculinity and militaristic international community whilst also taking into account the unique local gender construction that must be acknowledged in any decision on intervention" (Ibid:183).

In contemporary history, particularly since the Cold War, international intervention has been guided by a principle of state sovereignty—territorial integrity, where states are allowed the, "right to conduct themselves as they please within the confines of their own borders, with self-determination for nationalist groups running a poor second to governmental authority" (Ibid:185). In this situation territorial integrity has tended to overwhelmingly trump human rights, something which Julie Mertus (2000) proposes should not be an issue, as, "the principles of 'territorial integrity' and 'human rights' need not conflict: the former cannot be had without the latter and the realization of human rights can support the integrity of territory" (Rodgers, 2001:186). While some would suggest that human rights and territorial integrity should not come into conflict, history has shown that the two often do, and in this conflict the integrity of territory tends to trump human rights, with the situation of women and gendered abuses fitting into this trumped side.

According the Rodgers, "Rape as a war crime is not incidental; it is a calculated feature of ethnic cleansing and the destruction of enemy moral. 'It routinely serves a strategic function in war and acts as an integrated tool for achieving military objectives" (Ibid: 188). As such, "rape in conflict must be understood as an abuse that targets women for political and strategic reasons" (Ibid: 189). In this understanding of rape in conflict one can begin to see how such act while constituting human rights abuses are also very much political acts, and thus, "potentially subject to intervention criteria" (Ibid: 191). However, framing rape which occurs during conflict as political as a strategy for intervention has its pitfalls also according to Rodgers with respect to, "the sensitivities of local communities regarding how to treat the victims and perpetrators of these crimes," can be adequately by the international community" (Ibid:192). This is on account, according to Rodgers, that, "where difference needs to be accounted for, the international community simply cannot operate effectively" (Ibid).

FEMINIST ETHICS OF INTERVENTION

Feminist intervention must be flexible and respond to cultural difference (Ibid: 191). While international intervention has tended to overlook the situation and rights of women and abuses against them, feminist intervention also comes with dilemma. In the eyes of the author feminists must, "decide whether they wish to defend a broad conceptualization of women's human rights or accept that some cultural context will fall outside of Western feminist ideas on fairness and justice" (Ibid). This dilemma which faces feminists, with respect to intervention signifies the conflict between local and international facing the inclusion of feminist agenda in conflict intervention and action. Along the same lines as Snyder et al. (2006), Skjelsbaek rejects biological theories on wartime rape, which link sexual violence during conflict to male biology (essentialist position) or simply the war itself (structuralist position); instead taking a social constructionist approach. Taking a socialist constructionist, "provides a framework for conceptualizing the ways in which femininity, masculinity and violent political power struggles interact in constructing the meaning of sexual violence in armed conflict" (Skjelsbaek, 2012: 140).

The political psychology of war rape from a socialist constructionist position understands such violent acts of human rights abuses as centrally linked to gender relations, norms, and constructions. In this we are prompted to conclude that, "war rape...be understood as a violent relationship in which the perpetrator is masculinized and the victim feminized. In this process, other identities linked to the masculinized perpetrators and the feminized victims are sexualized in a hierarchical fashion, where power follows masculinization and powerlessness follows feminization" (Ibid). Understanding the political psychology of war from a socialist constructionist position coincides with the author's position on understandings of the Bosnian conflict, holding that too often women are understood to be, "passive victims of war," who are essentialized and, "portrayed as belonging to the 'women, children and elderly' group who are vulnerable and in need of protection" (Ibid: 8).

Skjelsbaek differs from other scholars on the topic of the Bosnian war and sexual violence whom hold sexual violence that occurred, to be a tool of war. According to the author, such positions understand the female body to be, "yet another battlefield where ethnic conflict can be fought, where a woman's sexual identity—in conjunction with her political and religious national identity—is the main target for the actions being carried out" (Ibid: .25). Skjelsbaek focuses not on the intent of sexual violence but rather the outcome, arguing that, "the use of rape in war alters the intersectionality between gender and other political identities" (Ibid: 141)

For Skjelsbaek in the case of Bosnia, "rape...sexualizes other gendered as well as non-gendered identities for political purposes and thereby alters the ways in which masculinization and feminization are perceived" (Ibid). For example, in the Bosnian case, Skjelsbaek through data collected from interviews uncovered that wartime rape in Bosnia impacted and infringed upon the respondents' social identity, with one aspect disrupted being ethnicity and the other gender, what Skejelsbaek refers to as "dual identity violation" (Ibid:142). With respect to ethnicity a narrative of the survivor materializes, coming from the, "absence of guilt, support from family members, and active engagement in getting their perpetrators convicted" (Ibid: 143). On the other hand, the narrative which emerges surrounding gender is one of a victim, "characterized by feelings of guilt and shame, hiding their stories from immediate family members, and bodily pains and immobility" (Ibid: 142). Thus, despite enduring the same act, the outcome of such an act differs, whether expressed through ethnicity or gender.

According to the author the situation of rape and sexual violence which occurred during the years of the Bosnian war cannot be fully understood without first, "understanding how gender relations—that is, notions of femininity and masculinity—are socially constructed in direct and symbolic social interactions," in this setting, giving attention to the, "interaction between gender and politics of identity" (Ibid: 4). Meaning, that it is the manner in which women's victimization is formed during and after war is vital to the understanding of, "the ways in which sexual violence has political impacts" (Ibid: 25). Ethnicity is commonly understood to be the dominant theme and reason behind the Bosnian war, as it was, "through the conflict that ethnic differences came to define friend and foe, compatriots and enemies, perpetrators and victims" (Ibid: 28). It is this overriding account of ethnic conflict and tension surrounding analysis of the Bosnian war which, according to the author, minimizes the place of gender in the situation. Skjelsbaek argues that, "While it is clear that the women who suffered war rapes in Bosnia were targeted on the basis of their ethnicity, it is also clear that they were targeted with this particular form of violence by men because they were women (Skjlesbaek, 2012:36). As a result of this, Skjelsbaek found in the Bosnian case that, "In general [...] gender roles have become more polarized by nationalism and war, [as such] rape against women in the war zone can therefore be regarded as an attack on current, and future, family formation, [with] men...called to fight and/or be killed, whereas women...are set to keep the home fires burning...com[ing] to represent stability" (Ibid:36-37).

Women's rights are human rights. For example, when playing a game of soccer and only half the team is allowed to participate, that team will never win. Many ethnic groups come to Canada where parts of their culture deny women equal space and literally suppresses them because they believe it's a man's world. We cannot change the world over night. However, step-by-step, we must empower women and actively introduce and execute programs educating men how to respect women and their right to equal space.

Chapter 5: Peacekeeping

In the year 1992 a peacekeeping monument was erected in Ottawa to honour the soldiers of Canada who have participated in UN missions throughout the world.

The UN pursued two approaches to peacekeeping; the first approach, military observers were sent to observe and report the status of truce. The second approach, deploy combat units in a ceasefire zone between warring forces. Canadian troops have served in both contexts, furthermore providing arm control verification, technical support, communication, and provide humanitarian assistance in hot spots. They have also participated in missions not sponsored by the UN.

Early into the year 2005, there seemed to be little that was good news regarding the legitimacy of that August body known as the United Nations (U.N.), a series of crises appeared to inflict serious damage to the moral authority of the organization. Events such as, the "Oil-for-Food" scandal involving no less than the Secretary General's own family; the involvement of U.N. officials in child prostitution rings; and the inability of the U.N. to respond to the tsunami crisis in Southeast Asia with strength of purpose, have served to inflict great injuries to the reputation of the U.N. as a model human rights resource. Indeed, in the wake of the U.N.'s failures in other countries like Rwanda and the Sudan, it almost appeared as if the U.N. was not only morally bankrupt, but had become a "craven shell" of what it once was. Thankfully, however, not all was as bad as this picture depicts; for there were points of light that could easily be identified and studied. One of these that stand out from the others is the tradition of "Peacekeeping," first begun by the former Prime Minister of Canada, Lester B. Pearson. Peacekeeping is a subject dear to the hearts of many Canadians, and it is a subject which is extremely close and personal to me. For this reason, in this section of book, I will discuss the nature and role of peacekeepers, the history and effects of the Bosnian conflict, and how the intervention in Bosnia was the key to achieve peace and hope in Bosnia today.

WHAT ARE PEACEKEEPERS, AND WHAT DO THEY DO?

To the average person, it would seem a simple question with a simple answer. Peacekeepers "keep the peace." They stand on a line that separates life and death for those trapped in an area of violent and unresolved conflicts. In this light, keeping the peace seems a relatively simple task. It is important to keep a level head, keep things honest, and treat all sides fairly. This is something your average police officer or school principal is trained to do. Yet these types do not represent the men and women who are used as peacekeepers. It is the soldiers–men and women who have been trained to kill in countless ways, to fight with a devious intelligence, and at breathtaking speed–who are asked to step in between feuding peoples from alien cultures; even though the adversarial parties have little or no incentive to listen to or respect the blue-helmeted interlopers in their midst. When a soldier is trained to kill, they are, in a sense, mechanized. They are desensitized, and that soft human part where sympathy and empathy reside, is removed. For all intents and purposes, they are somewhat disturbed; actually, psychopaths, in a sense. Yet, for peacekeeping missions, they are asked to re-sensitize themselves; actually, to strip away those parts of the personality which, in a combat zone, would otherwise keep them alive. This is a task that is very difficult. Above and beyond that, they are saddled with ridiculous, and at times suicidal, use-of-force restrictions. They are hampered by their lack of intensive human relations training. Potential enemies surround them day and night. Yet these men and women are still expected to carry out their assigned missions.

Peacekeeping is a way to help countries torn by conflict create conditions for sustainable peace. UN peacekeepers-soldiers and officers, civilian police officers and civilian personnel from many countries-monitor and observe peace processes that emerge in post conflict situations and assist ex-combatants to implement the peace agreements they have signed. Such assistance comes in many forms, including confidence-building measures, power sharing arrangements, electoral support in strengthening the rule of law and economic and social development.

Peacekeeping focuses on three key areas of responsibility. First, there is the protection of humanitarian operations where the international community will attempt to alleviate massive human suffering. In this case, humanitarian aid must be protected from those involved in armed violence. Second, when a ceasefire is signed, peacekeepers are brought in to ensure that whatever accord has been drafted will be respected by the different sides. In these situations, the peacekeepers' presence is there to encourage opposing forces to withdraw, so that negotiations can proceed smoothly. Third, peacekeepers liaise with third-party civilian organizations to facilitate the monitoring of human rights issues, the staging of elections, as well as the development of secure environments sans, the onerous task of integrating combatants back into civilian life. In all cases, peacekeepers represent the "go to" linchpin contact point without which, none of the aforementioned objectives would be feasible.

At times, the operational mandate of peacekeepers can be adjusted in order to deal with special circumstances. For example, following the final cessation of hostilities in Bosnia, just before U.N. forces orchestrated the return of refugees to their homes, the homes of displaced Serbian refugees were being burned down. This was said to be one of many non-military acts of aggression that continued for years, despite the formal end of the war. According to Lieutenant Colonel Peter Devlin, commanding officer of the 890th Strong Battle Group of CFB Petawawa, SFOR (Stabilization Force) began the operation in response to the way the peace process was being blatantly obstructed. Arson does not require a group, and is often the act of a single individual. Due to this, it is very hard to pinpoint a leadership driven system and to address the issue in that manner. What was needed was an entirely different way of approaching the problem. To that end, Operation Nero was designed, and though unconventional, was very successful.

Operation Nero was less of a military operation and more of an intense psychological mission. Since most cases of arson were occurring at night, soldiers were equipped with night vision goggles, a fact that was obvious to civilians in the area. Further, patrols were dramatically increased at night. This included soldiers on foot, constant helicopter patrols equipped with millions of candlepower searchlights, and scouts in the nearby hills equipped with heat sensing equipment. Also, during the day, a large military presence was maintained, along with non-stop broadcasts warning against arson, and there were posters put up which emphasized that arson was an individual crime, and not an organized political act. These measures, combined, directly resulted in the end of the arson scourge that was threatening to derail the peace process.

Though there are standard operation procedures, and policies designed to limit peacekeeping activities, peacekeepers still find themselves having to improvise policy rather than just implement it. In order to give peacekeepers the flexibility they need to deal with given situations correctly, objectives were sometimes loosely framed. As of 1995, the Canadian peacekeepers in Bosnia had two major tasks. First, they had to provide a safe and secure environment for the local people; and, secondly, they were to provide humanitarian aid when necessary to those in need. With the help of ubiquitous, twenty-four-hour security surveillance, seven days a week, the soldiers on patrol were able to gather information on individuals and groups in need. The use of technology in this way was a key factor in the success of the peacekeeping mission.

Mr. Fraser was born February 25, 1946, in North Preston, Nova Scotia. After obtaining his high school education, Mr. Fraser decided on a career in the military and joined the army. In 1967, he accepted his first tour of duty to Cyprus followed by developments to Somalia, Rwanda, Bosnia and Golan Heights. In his very satisfying 34-year military career, Mr. Fraser achieved the rank of Command Chief Warrant Officer with the Canadian Forces. After his retirement he returned to Nova Scotia with his family. In an old interview on peacekeeping he said, "Every Canadian that goes on a mission makes a difference. It's a part of our make-up. You know, any place I've gone as a Canadian, we were well respected. Peacemaking makes it a little difficult because you're now going a different route.

MY HEROES, GONE BUT NOT FORGOTTEN

"A soldier of the legion lay dying in Algiers. There was a lack of women's nursing; there was a dearth of women's tears. But a comrade stood beside him, while his lifeblood ebbed away" Caroline Norton.

What people in general, whom we call "civilians," fail to realize is that in battle soldiers mostly react instinctively, and sometimes intuitively, to situations as these arise. In fact, this is what we are trained to do! In wartimes, soldiers normally "huddle" together when confronted with danger during a firefight, on patrol or guard duty, in an ambush operation or on combat assaults. Soldiering is the most extreme "team activity." Some of the most heart-wrenching lyrics I have ever come across is in the song "Lonely Soldier Boy." Soldiers practically worship their comrades. Among soldiers, there is true democracy, and true equality because these are the people who are always at the forefront of danger in war zones. We call this level of engagement the "Infantry" and here I share my experience in verse.

At the end, I am very proud, honoured, to have walked the earth with outstanding, selfless human beings, who will stand on guard for Canada bravely, without hesitations. Every moment, I thank God for this fantastic opportunity, it is a moment I will cherish until I go to the afterlife. I would like all Canadians, old and new to know them. We breathed the same air, shared the same tent, dug and slept in the same trench, went on morning runs and faced the same enemy. Men like these are hard to come by and are far and few in between this vast land we call Canada. They have set the bar high for Canadians and global conscience. My fallen heroes; those who I have walked the earth with and are now in the paradise of heroes:

Steve Young (1992)
Mike Blizzard (1995)
Joe Parsons (1998)
Robert Hodgson (1999)
Chuck Barnsley (2000)
Eric Gendron (2001)
Jay Morin (2002)
Robert Short (2003)
Rick Nolan (2005)
John Predo (2014)
Alex Hogan (2014)
Ernie Hall (2016)
As we remember, my heroes that paid the ultimate sacrifice.

ROBERT HODGSON

(Demigod of the Land and Nature, Wisdom, Compassion, Fatherhood)

In the spring of 1985, Robert Hodgson was appointed the Company Sergeant Major (CSM) of November coy, 3RCR. A warrior no doubt, he stood 5 feet 7 inches, he was an iconic figure, very powerful. He approached life very calm yet stern and he never demanded respect it was naturally given to him. I was now a sr. private and selected as a member of the company quartermaster staff, which spelled out responsibility. The Company Quartermaster (CQ) staff for rv85 was dispatched to Wainwright, Alberta in May comprising of Pte. Salick, Cpl. Pinset, CQ Gallant and the CSM. We were there to set up camp for the company, as we would be there for the next 4 months. It was the second day and Pinset went into Wainwright to fill the water buffalo, CQ gallant went to purchase and collect rations, while the CSM went to one of his long drawn out meetings on the Hill, and I was assigned to dig the company size latrine. After 4 hours of digging all alone, the CSM had finished his meeting and now standing over the latrine and observing my work, while I was digging he asked, "will you finish this before the main body arrives"? I replied, "Yes Sir," and he said to me "you are in very high spirits." "Always sir, I love my job and I love the life." All of a sudden, he said "get out, I am jumping in," I got out and he jumped in and began digging. He stated to me, "the rank does not matter so long as the job gets done."

At that moment I realized what a powerful organization that I am part of. Can you imagine, a company sergeant major, getting dirty with a Pte., digging a company size latrine, and no questions asked? At the end of the day, the latrine was constructed and I went on with Pinsent later that evening to construct a company size shower. I was so motivated, that this moment will last with me until I go into the next world. RV 85 came to an end, and in September 1985, new troops came into November company, a group of impressive young men. I always looked forward to moments like this when the new recruits came into the infantry family. The CSM always used to say to me, "Salick, so long as you're having fun, stay with us, when the fun is gone, then you can go." I often wondered, what was the background of the young men who will commit their life to the infantry. Quite clearly, the first qualities are as follows; the young man who is not afraid of any challenges, one who has respect for self and others, is honest, and one who believes in tradition and finally one who is very patriotic.

In the spring of 1987 he was still my CSM., he called me in his office, I was all banged up, a nine-inch plate in left arm with a few screws holding it together. I was strung out on pain killers. At his office, he asked me to have a seat. While in conversation he asked, "what would you like to do? Would you like to go to another trade or stay with us?." I replied, "sir, what happened to me was a bump on the road, I would like to stay in the infantry because my family is right here." He said, "good, that's what I wanted to hear. We will look after you." He continued, "is there anyone you would like to assist you in your rehabilitation?" I said, "sir, Pte. Kevin Greig has already started assisting me, sir." He replied, "Scotty is a good one." I said, "thank you sir," and that was it. We had a saying, "live or die for the VRI," this was my intent. Fifteen years after that conversation I continued to serve infantry. If not for my injuries, I would still be there until death.

I recall the day in late June in 1988, when we were all called to the junior ranks to say farewell, thank you, and goodbye. He spent a good 15 minutes talking about women and family, and how to be respectful men by giving them their space. From then until now, I have travelled many countries and I have listened to many professors, journalists, commentators, and the words are so pretentious but his words were very sincere. This is an individual who never had a college or university education, he learned his values from his upbringing, he became a great leader, and a greater human being.

Mrs. Sherrill Hodgson:

Bob always wanted to be in the military growing up. Bob was very creative, he used to paint, write poems, draw, he was a photographer, he did everything, carpentry, he made my girl's bedrooms with chisels, no power tools or anything. He also did gardening, he won a prize for his gardening in Gagetown in the 90s (after they left Winnipeg). Bob wasn't an emotional type person, but when he came home he would be himself. Our daughter Cassandra would be in her crib, Bob would come home, look in her crib and pull away her blankets to see if she had grown.

He came home in 1998 from Bosnia for tests, he went into the hospital on the Wednesday, they called us in on the Friday, they informed us that Bob was suffering from terminal cancer. Bob had the infantry mentality where he would put his job before his sickness. He always said, I quit Bosnia, he felt that he didn't have the chance to go to Bosnia. It was hard on him to be where he couldn't do his job. There was a parade at 1 RCR, the CO said, "we are here to welcome the RSM back," they all clapped, threw their berets in the air, which they don't usually do. She didn't tell Robert of the event, she just showed up and she was brought to tears.

My girls loved the idea of the Airborne, one was in junior high and one was in high school, they each had a teacher who had derogatory comments about the Airborne. Cassandra stood up in class and said, "you don't know what you're talking about, you don't know what these men and women go through." The other one went to the counsellor to complain, thereafter the teacher apologized to Rayleen. My daughters and I do not see him the same way soldiers do. Soldiers, see him as someone who is an iconic figure. There must've been jumping going on with the Airborne school. The young driver kept going on and on about what a great guy their dad was, then she said, "you try living with him for 18 years." Mrs. Hodgson laughed about it.

His dream was to retire in a cabin, he loved the outdoors, he didn't believe in camping in a trailer, never with propane, you don't camp unless you sleep on the ground. He built his own canoe, a cedar strip canoe, hatches at each end like a kayak so you could put things in it. She lightheartedly remarked, "I will come visit you every six months."

When he was sick, we did an eight-day trip in a canoe, the Rideau Canal from Kingston to Ottawa, did all the locks. She was hoping he would take a friend but he took her instead.

One week prior to his death he received a medal from the governor general. After his death, the 'Dropzone' in Trenton was named in his honour and one of the camps in Bosnia was also named in his honour.

Dave Kearly Reflects...

An outdoorsman, born a century too late...lol. From throwing machetes, axes, and having defaulters there to retrieve them, to out shooting troops with his flint lock while they had C1s (new rifles).

Bobby was the ultimate frontiers man, a fine man, husband, mentor, and warrior taken from us too early.

ROBERT SHORT

(Demigod of the Land, Strength, Love, Wits)

Robert Short, this brother of mine, was an exceptional human being and an awesome soldier; we met on our leadership course of fall 1994 and shared the same room, Salick, Short, Thibault and Twaddle. Rob was very laid back, always-approached situations with a cool head, always rational and thoughtful in his approach. We would be bellowing words of command in the middle of the night, while the rest of the base sleeps. Rob would always seek out the best for the team. I remember, while given a task to dig and construct a trench on a rock sheet, while I was cursing the officer among the boys, he observed the ground and realized our trench will be completed within two hours. It was like magic, about two feet in front, a sheet of rock was into the ground, he then suggested we dig around the rock and free it from the soil, that will be our depth and we can go deeper we then take the piece that is rooted out of the soil and place it strategically in front for protection.

Humanitarian Run:

After completing the Ironman, I received a phone call stating that my favorite cousin who resides in Trinidad needed a kidney transplant and they were raising funds to cover the medical bills. I immediately suggested that my contribution will be a 500 kilometer run in 5 days to raise funds and awareness. I approach Rob and I said to him, would you like to come to Trinidad with me to participate in a fundraiser? He replied, "I would love to but I have my family however, I will do whatever I can." I replied, "Thank you, Rob." I mentioned my departure date and so forth which was about maybe about a week away. Immediately Rob gave me a bag of goodies. It had energy gels for runners, gatorade bars, and a short list of nutritious foods that I should consume while doing this run. I thanked him once again and I said, "I hope one day, maybe you and your family can travel to Trinidad." He smiled and said, "Thank you Slick."

Newspaper Articles from the Humanitarian Run; 100 kilometers per Day

Prague Marathon:

Our contingent team will participate in the Prague marathon, Czech Republic in the spring of 2001. Our Canadian contingent team was now in Bosnia doing our duty of maintaining peace and providing humanitarian aid whenever we can in "No man's land." After one training session they selected the names for the runners to participate in the Prague marathon and my name was one of them.

We arrived in Prague, myself and Rob Short, were assigned the same hotel room. Most of the team were rather young. For example, Jay Morin (RIP) was 19 years old. After dinner, myself and Rob decided to go and collect our numbers and package from the Prague marathon organizers. After a lite dinner (at one of the restaurants, I fell in love with the waitress, ha, ha. Of course I flirted with her for a little bit), Rob looked at me and shook his head, saying, "Slick what are you doing?" It was all in good fun though. The waitress was very warm towards us because we were Canadians. I must add, many countries we travel to, people are always warm to us. They know of the good job we do as Canadian peacekeepers.

After dinner, we made it back to the hotel. We relaxed for a bit and decided to go to the mall nearby, to sight see and do a little bit of shopping. Of course, I had purchased a couple of cans of Red bulls, they definitely give me wings, ha, ha. It was about 10pm in the evening now and we were in the hotel lobby, Rob had tried several times to contact his wife without any luck. I said to Rob, "I will stay with you until you get in touch with your wife, then I will go out." (I am a single man so I am allowed to go out and have fun whereas Rob is a married, responsible, respectable man). He mentioned to me in the past, maybe I should get a girlfriend or a wife, maybe I will be more responsible, ha ha. While sitting in the lobby, I started to ponder what a deep and sincere love Robert had with his wife.

It was now at least 11-11:30pm, I said to Rob, "I am going to take off, wake me up at about 5am." As I was about to leave, he got through to his madam, he opened the door to the phone booth and gave me the thumbs up. I walked to the front of the hotel and I was very happy for Rob because he made contact with his wife. Outside the hotel I stood leaning on the wall, reflected and concluded to myself, "what a relationship, such a deep love. This kind of love will make the lovers of the world envious of sincere romantic love. What a human being, my hero." Thereafter, I walked out to one of the clubs and I was gone until at least 4:30 in the morning. At the hotel, I shaved and showered hoping not to wake up Rob. I heard Rob's voice, "morning Slick, I will wake you up at 5:30," and I went to bed.

We were now on our way to the race, my two Red bulls in my hands and I was good to go. The race began at 8:00. At the start point, we were at least 1.5 kilometers away from the start line. There were so many runners I was dumbfounded. What was different though, we had to run on cobalt stones for quite a while. It was my first time running on such an uneven surface.

Myself and Rob were now at the 14th kilometer mark and we saw those African runners at the 21 kilometer point and they were flying. They were built like sticks; they were just flying like the wind. Rob looked at me and said, "Slick, I will see you at the end," and he picked up his pace. I said, "See you." My purpose was to complete the race, I had started 1.5 kilometers behind, with thousands of people ahead of me, I knew that I would not win the race or have a good finishing time (personally I like winning, given the proper time, space, and training, I would win). My early morning prowls and the sun did not do me any favors.

Together with Robert we completed our leadership course (ISCC), we ran the Ottawa half marathon; the military Ironman, and the Prague marathon. Rob had a wife and two young children; here is someone I assumed God would be just to him; a loving compassionate human being. Strange was the day when I left 3RCR, Petawawa. Rob was the base orderly Sgt. I presented him with a poem I wrote about us, the Infantry, and I said, "I will go upstairs and give a copy of the poem to Lt. Col. Thompson," because I had soldiered with him in Germany during the cold war. On my way back to where Rob was standing, he called out "Slick you cannot just leave us, what's your plan?" I replied, "as you know, my injuries are hindering me, I will go to university to finish my degree and come back." He said, "sounds like a good plan." We hugged each other, and I remember saying: "Rob, thank you for your advice and friendship over the years. Take care of the family; there isn't any better human being that I know, brother." I said "good bye." He replied: "There isn't any goodbyes with us, 3RCR will always be your home. Just come back when you finish your education, Pro Patria"

CHUCK BARNSLEY

(Demigod of Strength)

Warrant Officer Chuck Barnsley, a soldier's soldier, tough as nails, an unbelievable human being and a family man. Ironman 2000 is taking place and all teams have commenced training. 3RCR selected their first team, with Cpl Salick as the store's man, which means I will have all the equipment ready for the daily training. I believed, after 6 weeks of training, the team looked trim and fit. Warrant officer Barnsley said to me "Slick, I would like you to run with the team tomorrow morning because I need some company on the run." The run was Friday morning, 50 kilometers, with 50 pounds of kit in your rucksack. I said, "No problem." He looked at me and his eyes opened as though surprised at my reply.

The run started at 0800 hours. The Ironman team accounted for, with kit. Refreshments would be available at the end of the run. As we started the run he said to me: "Slick, stay with me, we are like old engines; we will go forever while the young soldiers will take off at a fast pace. Verner, Short, and Cushman will push them to the end." After 6 hours of running, the event was finished. We had left a few young lads behind as he stated some withered away. Rob Short was magnificent, inspiring the lads along with Sgt. Cushman. The Warrant Officer (W.O.), looked at me and asked: "Slick, why did you not try out for the team"? I replied, "I was supposed to go on course and it was full, so I opted to be the store's man for the team." I stated, "thank you W.O. for the opportunity; I would love to compete in the Ironman in the future." Life is strange, we ran that day together. In the early hours next morning, Warrant Officer, Chuck Barnsley, had passed away. The Ironman was now a week away, Rob Short approached me, "Slick, would you like to do the Ironman?" I replied, "I would love to." I asked Cpl. Price to accompany me on a run from Petawawa to Pembroke and back, with 50 pounds in the rucksack, portage a canoe from 3rcr to the Petawawa River, and I did some canoeing with his instructions. I was now ready to compete in the Ironman 2000.

What was amazing was the fact that Warrant Officer Barnsley had created a training program where in 6 weeks the Ironman team will execute their best performance. This is an infantry solider with all this knowledge, experience, and wit. He is someone who will run from his house, 20 kilometers to reach the base. After he would arrive at the base he would participate in a run with his platoon, maybe 10, 15, or even 20 kilometers. Yes, he was part machine, part human, part God; a demigod.

My fellow heroes in the quarters where I lived, Cory, Ricky and Alex, gave me their support. Although feeling a bit uneasy, after the Ironman dinner, the evening before the competition, we decided to go to the warehouse (club) to relax. We were there until 2 am; I had to be ready for the competition at 4 am. I made sure my rucksack was packed and ready to go alongside my uniform. I overslept, and Alex came and woke me up. Then Cory drove me to the 1RCR building where all of the teams were gathering. I was 5 minutes late, and I said to my boys, "I am just going for a long jog." Rob Short came over to me and asked, "Slick, are you okay?" He made sure I was ready for the race. He continued, "You never trained for the race, so all I want you to do is finish the race so we could have a team victory. On another day with training, I know you can win this competition." (N.B. The Ironman Legs: Leg 1- run 38km with 30lbs on your back; Leg 2- portage a canoe of 75lbs with a 40lb weight on your back for 4.5 km over rough terrain; Leg 3- canoe for 7.5km; Leg 4- run 5.5km with 45lbs on your back.)

Rob said, "Slick, just pace yourself; remember some of these teams were training for roughly between 4 to 6 months. We do not want a hero." I replied, "Thank you Rob for your confidence in me. I will see you at the end." When the race ended, I finished in 7hours and 47 minutes, and there were competitors still on the trail. I was very happy to see RSM Grattan (another iconic figure with the RCR's and Airborne) at the end, where he shook my hands and said: "Well done." Rob and the rest of the team shook my hands and congratulated me. Honestly, it felt good with a lot of pain. Also, I wished RSM Hodgson had been there to see me finish this race because he was truly my mentor, the person I looked up to greatly (iconic).

Eric Gendron

(Demigod of Hope and Youth)

Eric Gendron, we called him "Blue Eyes." He was 20 years old when he came to our unit to get a bit of purpose in his life. He was so young and full of energy, the youngest in my section. He was the life of the section. We would come back from a hard day's training and the boys would be exhausted. We did this training over and over for every tour, the four phases of war, preparation for the unexpected when one considers warfare. Eric would come up with a joke, tell a story, and imitate one of us or the sergeant major to perfection. We would all have a laugh. I never really saw him in an exhausted state. His energy transcended all exhaustion throughout the section. He was a very talented young man, and at that age he was willing to serve in the toughest trade in the military, the Infantry.

Mr. Gendron (Eric's Father) Recollects...

"Eric did the same with his basic training and battle school instructors. He portrayed them all better than they themselves could. He had energy to spare since birth. Maybe because his mother did high impact aerobics until her 7th month of pregnancy. Wondering now if he ever imitated me or my wife."

"He was the subject of a study at Carleton University in Ottawa. When he was born, my wife smoked and they asked if they could include him in their study to see the effects of smoking on the child. They were so intrigued by him that they followed him until he was 18. Soon after birth they would toss him in the air and to each other while standing a few feet apart... Guess what? No notion of fear whatsoever. So what you saw in him he was born with."

"That might help you understand why he was so full of energy. Always was the life of the party. Not to be a show off, only to have fun."

"After his death, his brother Chris, 18 months older, and his sister Laurie, 8 years older, both joined the Canadian Forces to follow in his footsteps. Both are Sergeants, Chris a LCIS Tech at CFJSR in Kingston, and Laurie a Supply Tech at Canadian Military Training Centre in Wainwright. Both have been in 14 years, and Laurie signed up on Eric's birthday, July 11th, 2002. Chris signed up on Valentines day, 2002."

"I thought about you many times and wondered what had become of you. I can assure you that the high esteem you held for Eric was mutual. He would have followed you anywhere without ever doubting the outcome. If you could earn his trust and respect, you had him "Hook, line, and sinker!" You did just that."

"We are both retired now and spend most of our time camping and travelling in the summer and spending the winter months in Florida."

"You also said something that hinted at his loyalty and how much he cared about his section buddies."

"The thing that did amaze me the most was that you took the time to come out and "Show your support" for one of your soldiers when someone else was in the process of throwing him under the bus. Not that he did not deserve it, but you were there for him. That is why you were the first to know on the army side."

"Over the course of 18 months in Pet, he brought most of the section, one or two at a time to meet us and his civilian buddies."

"Like in an infantry section, it is the whole section that makes it what it is, not the leader or its soldiers individually. So even if our current leaders are not the greatest, the people of this country will carry it through."

Salick Continues...

On several occasions we will converse one on one, we will bring up ideas of political and social setbacks that prevent Canada from becoming a greater nation. What was interesting, as infantry soldiers, we did not really discuss politics and development because we would leave that for the politicians to make the decisions for a greater Canada. He would suggest to me, "why don't you get out of full time service, join the reserves, and pursue university education." He was so young but also very wise; he saw a potential or ability that I would not have even begun to entertain.

He suggested that I should get involved in social and community development with the Government because, as he put it, "people like you can make a difference." I would reply, "Eric, young blood, I love this job; where in Canada do they pay you to stay fit, where we do the extreme, at times running 50 kilometers with 50 pounds on our backs? We will go out in the world and protect the defenseless women who are abused, left unprotected by the corrupt governments in the world. "This is what I live for, Young Blood." Eric was selected as our driver for the upcoming tour to Bosnia-Herzegovina in 2001. The section trained hard and we came together nicely with regular and reserve (militia) soldiers. Eric lived in Ottawa not too far from base Petawawa. He received a weekend pass and went home to visit his parents and girlfriend. Maybe too excited, he left base Petawawa in a rush without his vehicle license. While in Ottawa, he probably had a little falling out with his young lady. On his way back to Petawawa, he stopped in Pembroke about 20 kms away from Base Petawawa. On his way to the base, the Pembroke Police doing their job, pulled him over. He was driving under the influence of alcohol. He gave me a call 0200 hours in the morning to pick him up because he could not drive his vehicle.

Not a problem. The weekend was over; he was given a court date before our tour to Bosnia. I attended the court date for his hearing where he received six months of probation.

As I was in my dress uniform, I immediately stated to the judge: "Your Honor, thank you. I will make sure he respects the probation as we are leaving for Bosnia for 6 months, and I will be his section commander." The judge replied: "Thank you, young man." At the court house I met Eric's parents; they were a really nice couple. I promised Eric's father that I would look after young Eric.

What is amazing when I look back is that he saw things that I never saw because I was so caught up in the infantry world. He was young and full of ideas, he envisioned a greater Canada. The weekend before we were to be deployed in Bosnia-Herzegovina he was given a weekend pass to visit his family to say good bye. He never came back as he was tragically killed by a drunk driver in Ottawa.

MY BROTHERS WHO STOOD ON GUARD WITH ME, AND ARE STILL HERE:

Kevin Greig
Cory Daly
Rick Mckewan
Ali Nehme
Richard Moreno
Sean Bohrson
David Somers
Ben Brown
Todd Watson
Scott Casey
Alan Edison
Nathan Ferguson
Onek Adyanga
Pat Greene
Vijay Seeloch
Anthony Jones
Wayne Evans
Chris Hancock
Jim Lahey
Steven Parsons
David Kearly
Rick Keizer

Ali Nehme (left) and Cory Daly (right) on Remembrance Day.

CORY/RICKY/ALI

These three young men I call the musketeers, whenever you see them, they are always together. We all occupied the same section in our living quarters/shacks. They were three brothers you could depend on if you were ever in need of anything. We lived there together for five years. For example, after our first Bosnian tour, we got back in January 1999, myself, Ricky, and Cory, made a trip to Trinidad for its carnival. Simultaneously, Ali had family commitments, therefore he did not make the trip with us. Even until this day we keep in touch because of the bond that was created.

In the words of Cory Daly (2013), "It is hard to be ordinary when you were once extraordinary." From 1982-2002, I lived a life that was extraordinary, fast and full of excitement, without regrets.

These are examples of some heroes, who made the ultimate sacrifice. My question now is to you, old and new Canadians who sit on their buttocks, expecting handouts from the state to provide for them without making an effort to contribute to the state. Also, I want to reach out to the criminal minds who constantly want to manipulate hard working people by robbing them of their hard earned liberties. I hope this message will reach you: we live in the greatest multicultural country in the world, and I ask you to contribute 10% of what my heroes gave. To think, I started as a boy in 3RCR and after 20 years I am now man. I have walked the Earth with the finest human beings; I am truly blessed to have met these wonderful, humble souls.

When I think of my heroes, they have set the benchmark of patriotism, and with that I could only ask of old and new Canadians alike to give at least 10% of what my heroes gave.

The members of the RCR are the apotheosis of patriotism; they are the majestic, selfless, kind, peaceful, caring and compassionate human beings who are willing to give up everything for this great nation. They are men who are disciplined and well trained for war, and as quickly as you flip a coin, they will give up everything and will not ask Canada for anything in return.

The life of the infantry soldiers is demanding and the work is beastly. Up at dawn, they train in extremely harsh conditions. By 1000 hours, the amount of work that they accomplished before the civilian world awakes it is mammoth. Furthermore, on average they live at least six months a year in the wild outdoors and they eat ration packs, while the civilian world is enjoying caviar and wine. They sleep in tents on cots and bivouac bags on the ground. Their legs are the major mode of transport and they carry their food, clothing, ammunition, water, and rest of their basic needs for survival on their backs in the harshest conditions.

These men train for war to maintain world peace and, in my humble opinion, that makes them extraordinary human beings. Some intellectuals will call them the poor boys in society, well, if they are poor and are willing to make the ultimate sacrifice, what sacrifice are you willing to make?

My brothers of war and peace, when my number is called, we will meet in the afterlife. Their voices ring in my head every day, their smiles, stern attitude, and mental and physical toughness linger in my mind, asking me never to give up on soldiering because they are with me and I am with them. I often feel that I am ready for the afterlife because my heroes are already there. Today, I walk among old and new Canadians who have no idea of the sacrifice "My Heroes" have made, and thus erasing their existential contributions and history. My brothers, I will wave farewell on this day while we will honour you and know about your contributions, greatness, conviction, true patriotism and loyalty to Canada. You will be immortal like the demigods in Greek mythology. You are my heroes, you are Canada's unsung heroes. We will meet again in afterlife.

When we stood together, we were God-like and free. We were powerful in our status and our mental belief because our brotherhood, our bond, could not be broken. Even in death, memories of my brothers make me stronger. As every day goes by, my thoughts are with them.

I am humbled to walk this Earth with Canada's finest, most loyal and patriotic human beings, the men of the RCR family. For twenty years I lived a dream. I never wanted to leave, but God had other plans for me, and quite clearly because of them I made an attempt to understand war, peace, and the selflessness demonstrated by my brothers in arms. They have taught me so much, and by their teachings have saved a lost soul on this Earth. They gave me a purpose, a belief in an ideology of social justice, far greater than most people will ever understand. They taught me the willingness to give my life to protect and defend men, women and children who are abused, raped and massacred. They will not hesitate even a second to defend such people. I can say only in admiration what magnificent human beings they are. Mere words are not enough to express the feelings, thoughts and admiration I have for them.

I have demonstrated throughout my journey that Canada creates equal space for those who are willing to work and contribute to human development within our nation and globally. The Canadian culture is a community-oriented culture that is about kindness, giving and selflessness, and this culture is clearly alive in the East Coast of Canada.

Throughout this book, I presented parts of the life of the infantry soldier on UN/NATO/SFOR missions with some of my heroes. I saw my role as an individual relaying a message to make this country greater. My heroes have given everything; hence, I would like Canada to recognize them as demigods equal to the demigods of Greek mythology, Hercules, Achilles, and Hector. We cannot deny them their greatness or overlook their great contributions not only to Canada but also globally. You will live forever, my RCR family. Continue your great work nationally and globally.

You are the most powerful human beings in our society, you are demigods, the best of the best, and you will live forever through your deeds by protecting global humanity,

They were so powerful that being around them inspired you to do what appeared impossible to most human beings.

Every step that you make God watches over you, because you are his angels on this Earth.

I never walked the Earth with Achilles, Hector or Hercules; however, I took part in Ironman competitions, ran marathons, engaged in force marched, dug trenches, and endured pain and laughed aloud together with my comrades. These were not part of our DNA, but we drew inspiration from each other by breathing an air in which valor, compassion and humanity were the key words.

I am only a traveler and God allowed me to participate on this fantastic journey with you, the demigods of Canada at the close of the past century and into the new millennium.

They walked among us and we could not see them; they never asked for anything, but their influence is evident everywhere as their values remain a source of inspiration for all of us. They inspire and influence us to be great in whatever task is given to us, in war and peace.

These were humble souls willing to serve global humanity while we were too busy seeking out our own selfish needs.

How do we honour them properly? They are the nation's heroes and we must do what is fitting.

This book intends to do them justice by ensuring that their names and deeds will live on. This book demands that Canadians should embrace their heroes/ demigods.

I present to you the demigods of Canada; they are greater than life, and yet humble and kind.

Walking with my Canadian Heroes, I lived a Dream,

Honor them, know them, they will be forever young,

My Heroes, Canada's Heroes.

Pro Patria.

Photo provided by WO Seeloch of D.A. Salick at the Petawawa Museum.

A NEW BEGINNING

I lived a dream. On August 13, 2002, my last day as a soldier in the Canadian Forces, the book was closed on that chapter of my life. But it wasn't the end of the dream for me, it was a new beginning. The memories of my heroes, the demigods who protected and inspired me, spurred me on.

I was once blessed and honoured to walk the earth with the finest Canadian infantry soldiers. You will travel far and wide and you will not meet men like this - their kindness, selflessness, toughness and most of all, willingness to safe guard or protect global humanity. For 20 years I was willing to give my life, to protect my brothers as they would have done for me. In the theatre of war and peace, I would fall asleep from exhaustion, knowing that they would protect my life as I would theirs. Pro Patria.

> "The infantry isn't for everyone, it's for the few with guts of steel and who welcome death." – Salick
> "In the infantry pain is non-existent, because what we do is roll it up into a candy and swallow it, the mission must be accomplished." – Salick

WO Vijay Seeloch (front right) training in Yuma, Arizona.

Epilogue: Professor K. Atkinson (York University)

The military as an institution has historically been framed as serving three fundamental roles in the formation of nation states. The first task is that of guarding the national borders of nation states. Over historical time borders became the most important attribute defining the geometry of what a nation is. The essentialization of borders as the defining DNA of nation states has given rise to an ethnonational myth which has normalized for better or worse that nation states are discrete containers with primordial sacred objects, places and spaces. The role of national armies is to protect and defend this national construct. Vibrant young men and women are called up and in some countries are called upon to carry out the duty of defending the nation state. National anthems such as "O Canada" and "Star Spangled Banner" have celebrated the army as the honored defender of "home and native lands," "land of the free and home of the brave." The men and women who serve in the army are automatically bestowed the honor of patriots and heroes.

In its second role the military has been constructed as an ideological institution, in Marxist terms as part of the superstructure and in Weberian terms as part of the rational bureaucratic order with monopoly power over the use of force. The Military as an ideological bureaucratic institution is crucial to the way in which concepts such as order and authority are framed and become a part of the national character of modern nation states. Historically, it is in the military that young men first learned the meaning of order as felicitous obedience to what those in authority, or those who have concentrated the means of power in their hands present as order. This sense of order is architectural, it is what civilization is built on, in this sense order is an ontological property of civilization. The military is like a medieval guild with a monopoly over the social meaning of what order is. Young men and women in the military apprentice in learning the meaning and accepting this meaning of order. Young men and women learn to accept a hierarchal conception of order and authority even if it does not square with their better judgement. Although not every young men and women have entered military training and service in Canada those who have entered the military for training and to service the nation state are inculcated and hegemonized to uncritically accept a certain conceptualization and practice of what social order and fidelity to authority are. Here again, just like in the first function of the military articulated above, the majority of citizens automatically venerate the soldiers who faithfully carry out their duties in accordance with this weltanschauung as developed and prescribe by the military. This can be seen in the way military families and the wider society accepts casualties of soldiers in the act of service with solemn reverence. The death of the soldier is never accompanied by public grieving and waling; it is death of the highest order, if death has its "General Estates" then the death of the soldier is of the very first order – a nobility of death. Here is the last stanza from a poem immortalizing the death of Sir Robert Sale British military commander in the battle of Moodkee, India, 1845:

....
Yes, it is ours and thine to weep-
Yet are they tears of pride;
He sleeps the conqueror's chosen sleep,
The soldier's death he died.
A fame is his no fame can dim,
No time can never pale-
Who would not die and lived like him,
The brave Sir Robert Sale.

It is in the military as a bureaucratic ideological institution that the hero complex of the secular nation state is formed. The military has democratized the process of hero construction in the secular nation state. The pathway to become a hero is to join the military or the police force and this is open to all young people who aspire to serve the nation as well as their communities. Whether or not they aspire to be heroes is not of their choice or making, the hero title comes along with enlistment without regard to ascriptive characteristics or the utility of action/conduct in service. This of course opens up the military to the flaw of producing heroes on the cheap or diluting the hero attributes. Of course this is not equivalent to denying that true and worthy heroes are the product of military service. What is important however in a democratic society is for the military not to be given a free ride in its educational and ideological function in shaping minds and character of enlisted soldiers, nor to insulate the process of hero construction from democratic and public scrutiny.

The final function of the military that will be addresses is the military and soldering as opportunity for self-development, self-fulfillment, social capital and social mobility this is an important element from a sociological perspective. All nation states are built on certain myths among these are equal rights for all, equality before the law, citizenship as an equalizing force and equal access to material and social progress.

These myths became crystalized during the French bourgeois revolution in its battle cries of "Liberté, égalité, fraternité." The modern nation states as the manifestation of a macro-community of citizens has failed in implementing the battle cry of the French revolution for all citizens. The failure has not been by accidental, but by design. Nation states such as Canada has design-out through a policy of multiculturalism the virtues of "Liberté, égalité, fraternité" for all. The battle cries of the bourgeoisie in the 18th century were a necessary ideological instrumentality to defeat the ancient regimes and effect the liberation of the masses as a condition of hegemonizing bourgeois domination. The contradiction with this arrangement is that the battle cries of the bourgeois of "Liberté, égalité, fraternité" was janus faced. That is to say that the masses had to be freed from ancient bondage in order to be ultimately free to submit to their domination and submission under the modern bourgeois capitalist order.

This key contradiction has given rise to a new body of critical thinking under the label of Frankfurt school of critical theory Bourgeois modernism has been a colossal failure in implementing "Liberté, égalité, fraternité" for all. The modern bourgeois nation state has failed immigrants, working class, women, and ethnic minorities in their quest for freedom and social mobility. "Liberté, égalité, fraternité" have not been un-problematically permeable for immigrants, the working class, the under class and ethnic minorities within the civil life of the nation state. These social strata have had to discover alternative pathways for socioeconomic progress and social respectability.

The military and soldiering have provided a pathway for marginalized social strata to achieve socioeconomic material progress and a chance for social mobility that civil life in the institutional realm of the nation state have closed off to them or one reason or another. What is sociologically self-evident is that social inequality, social marginality, ethnic and racial divide are functional to the logic of progress and accumulation that underpin the materialist Darwinian culture of modernity which is the hallmark of the nation state. The military is one of the few institutions if not the only one of the modern nation state that is indifferent to socio-economic class background, racial and ethnic background or any other ascriptive attributes. At least so it appears from the advertisement it sends out to prospective recruits. Whereas these identities are determinative to one's life world opportunity in the civil life sphere of the nation state, there are dysfunctional to the workings and objectives of the military and soldiering as a profession. To the extent that the military and soldering are open for enlistment to all racial and ethnic groups the military as an institution is often seen as a deracinated institution. This might sound utopic, but all soldiers tend to believe this. This comes through very poignantly in Salick's book, "I Lived a Dream...." Salick has testified experientially to living a communitarian and deracinated experience in the military. Here are a few of the mottos of the Canadian military: *Unanimi cum ratione* ("united in purpose"), *Fortes soli, fortiores una* ("strong alone, stronger together"), *Vigilamus pro te* ("we stand on guard for thee"), *Pro patria* ("for country"); in the US army there is the motto and saying, *De opresso liber* ("to liberate the oppressed"), and "leave no man behind." There is a collectivist identity weltanschauung in the military that belies the worshiping of individualism in the civil life of Canadian and American societies.

The sociology of the Army and soldiering no doubt are complex subjects, given that the military is a complex institution with complex institutional logic which belies any attempt to reduce it to simplify reductionism. Soldiering while it is grounded in collectivist mentality and shared sociality, which collapses individual differences into collective "We" identity, soldiers are nevertheless individuals with complex motivations and psychology. "I Lived a Dream," is not a sociological treatise on the military and soldering. I Lived a Dream is a micro-level autobiographical look at how the Canadian military and soldering have shaped the live world opportunity and experience of an immigrant soldier. This micro-level narrative is combined with a meta-sociological analysis of the military as an institution with an opportunity cost that is Praeto optimal particularly for immigrants, the marginalized and those that are excluded from equal rights, equal benefits and inclusion in the civil life of the Canadian nation state.

I Lived a Dream portrays the journey of immigrant Derek Abdul Salick from an Island periphery to a first world nation state – Canada. Slick is acutely aware of the injustices in both geographies. The book tells the story of the hardship of Slick in his native Trinidad and Tobago. In the place of his birth Salick's life world was shaped or misshaped by race, class, consanguineous kingship considerations, cultural hybridity, colourtocracy. These factors and more are part of the fixed elements of the neocolonial experience that shape social existence to the detriment of normal live for post-colonial subjects. I Lived a Dream gives a peek into the struggle for survival of the many strategies and coincidences that make it possible for Salick to the escape socioeconomic limiting existence in Trinidad and Tobago.
Immigrating from one post-colonial geography to another postcolonial destination Canada, did not readily dissolve all of the postcolonial machinations. Canadian civil life possesses these postcolonial limitations that Salick sought to escape, but these are reflected in more rational justifying and subtle form. The one institution that opened it

gates to opportunities in Canada in an uncomplicated, but demanding manner for the immigrant seeking acceptance, community and equality of treatment, equality of result and a chance to escape from the definition of self, imposed under postcolonial conditions was the Canadian military. I Live a Dream venerates the Canadian military and soldiering for offering the underclass, immigrants and less fortunate the opportunity for economic progress and mobility and the possibility to reconstitute community and brotherhood while serving the nation.

I Lived a Dream taps into an aspect of the military, particularly the post war military that has been highlighted in numerous sociological studies on the military. The military has provided an option for economic opportunity to immigrants and racialized minorities to gain access to the economic pie in Canada and the US. In Canada during the interwar period it was poor working boys and men who joined up disproportionately more than boys and men from elite background to defend the nation. While clearly a sense of patriotic and nationalist duty was part of the motivation for serving, boys and men from working class and marginality backgrounds joined the military and became soldiers, because this was the only viable option for material survival and a sense of identity formation. Service in the military and soldering served those who survived their military service well. In the case of Canada in the post war era the men who came back from the war reintegrated back into the society material better off than they were before their military service. While each national military institution has its own history and narrative that may contradict the unique and individualized narrative that Salick paints in I Lived a Dream, what is undisputed in the case of the military and soldiering since the mid twentieth century in Canada and the US is the constructivist notion of the military as a mechanical solidaristic institution where the collective conscience, common adherence to norms, and brotherly love drown out the politics of difference.

I Lived a Dream is ultimately a narrative of the military and soldiering as a worthy pathway for those who want to find a sense of community; to have an opportunity for educational and material advancement; to challenge the boundary of one's physical endurance and to serve the nation at home and abroad. In this sense the military as an institution is contrast with the civil live of the nation where the pathway to these achievements is a lot more problematic. In the military racial identity, consanguineous kinship difference, class, gender and religious and sexual orientation are sublimated. What emerges from the military therefore is monothetic identity of the soldier, as deracinated, declassed, universal and cosmopolitan. As Salick laments in I lived a Dream, the focus on racism and racial identity politics as obstacles to material progress and personal growth in Canadian society is the work of intellectual idle doers. I Lived a Dream in one sense is a negation of the power of ascriptive attributes and identity assignments to determine the destiny of immigrants and racial minorities in postcolonial democratic liberal capitalist societies.

I Lived a Dream is a unique look at the military and soldering from the vantage point of a postcolonial immigrant soldier. There are no discussions of the military as instrument of war and destruction; or of the military as violators of human rights; or of the military as a mirror image of society in which racial inequality and discrimination are replicated. There are no discussions of soldiers accused of atrocities while serving the nation, or soldiers suffering the effect of post-traumatic stress disorder. I Lived a Dream is not about these realities. It is about the military and soldering providing a redemptive pathway for the migrating postcolonial immigrants seeking hope, a new home, a new commune, new horizons and new solidarity. All these things are presented as attainable in the military. Salick has lived the dream, because he can personally testify to achieving all these aspects in the Canadian military.

I Lived a Dream is a most intriguing book for the way in which it rejects conventional hegemonic narratives on such topics as immigration, nationalism, the military, hero construction, and role of ordinary individuals as change agents. The main character of the book, Salick, an immigrant from Trinidad and Tobago who is simultaneously the author of the book, overcomes the imputed social limitations of the immigrant in the first world country of Canada. Salick refuses to accept immigration as a limiting live world experience, or to accept immigration as a process of ethno-racial devaluation. Salick's sociological brilliance relates to his disavowal of racism and the immigrant as alien in his quest to make his life meaningful and socially consequential. Instead of race, racism, immigrant alien, and founding race, Salick sees a common humanity in all races. On the question of nationalism Salick disavows the socio-political significance of this analytical construct as a guide for human action; as a soldier in the Canadian military he has seen the worst of humanity played out on the battlefield of nationalism from the Cyprus, Greek-Turkish conflict to the killing fields of Bosnia. In all of this Salick articulates a narrative that emphasizes the cosmopolitan dimension of humanity. It is within this worldview that I Lived a Dream is a testimony to the potentiality of human beings to build true fraternal community where every person can be a hero. The book is a must read for those who dare to imagine alternative worlds.

REFERENCES

Ali, Rabia & Lifschultz, Lawrence. Why Bosnia? Writing On The Balkan War. (The Pamphleteer's Press: Connecticut, 1993)

Amnesty International. Bosnia-Hercegovina: How Can They Sleep At Night? Arrest Now! (Amnesty International: New York, 1997): 4.

Andrew Burtch (2010) ""Tact, diplomacy and an infinite store of patience" Cyprus and Canadian Peacekeeping," Canadian Military History: Vol. 19: Iss. 2, Article 7. Available at: http://scholars.wlu.ca/cmh/vol19/iss2/7

Aspen Community, The. Honoring Human Rights from Peace to Justice: Recommendations to the International Community. (The Aspen Community: Washington, 1998)

Bar-Tal, Daniel, and Yona Teichman. *Stereotypes and prejudice in conflict: Representations of Arabs in Israeli Jewish society.* Cambridge University Press, 2005.

Bryant, Rebecca. On the condition of postcoloniality in Cyprus. Indiana University Press, 2006.

Camp, Glen D. "Greek-Turkish Conflict over Cyprus." Political Science Quarterly 95.1 (1980): 43-70 Cavell 2004

Class Handouts. Just War Theory (Jus Ad Bellem Convention) York University, Pols 4210, 2003

Corwin, Philip. Dubious Mandate: A Memoir of the UN in Bosnia, Summer 1995. (Duke University Press: London, 1999)

Cousens, M. Elizabeth & Cater, Charles K. towards Peace in Bosnia: Implementing The Dayton Accord. (Lynne Renner: London, 2001)

Daalder, Ivo H. "Bosnia after SFOR: Options for Continued US Engagement." Survival: The IISS Quarterly, Winter 1997 - 1998. (Oxford University Press: London, 1997)

Denitch, Bogdam. Ethnic Nationalism: The Tragic Death of Yugoslavia. (University of Minnesota Press: Minneapolis, USA, 1996)

Denktash. R. The Cyprus Triangle: Publication info: London ; Boston : Allen & Unwin ; Nicosia, Northern Cyprus : K. Rustem & Bro., 1982.

Derrida, J. (1981). Positions. Chicago: The University of Chicago Press.

Denitch, Bogdan. Ethnic Nationalism. Minneapolis: University of Minnesota Press, 1994.

Fatic, Alexander. "The Nature of the Peace in the Former Yugoslavia: Heroes and Criminals – How To Distinguish Them?" Pols 4255: Issues in International   Human Rights Course Kit, Winter 2004. Toronto: York University, 2004.)

Fatic, Alexander. "The Nature of the Peace in the Former Yugoslavia: Heroes and Criminals – How To Distinguish Them?" Pols 4255: Issues in International   Human Rights Course Kit, Winter 2004. Toronto: York University, 2004.)

First Interim Report 1992 of the Varied Nations Commission of Breaches of Geneva Law in Former Yugoslavia. United Nations. 1992 (S/25274).

Gibbs, David. First Do No Harm: Humanitarian Intervention and the Destruction of Yugoslavia- Nashville: Vanderbilt University Press, 2009.

Giddens, A. 1992. Transformation of Intimacy Stanford. University Press

Goldstein & Pevenhouse. Reciprocity, Bullying, and International Cooperation: Time-series Analysis of the Bosnia Conflict. American Political Science Review / Volume 91 / Issue 03 / September 1997, pp 515 – 529.

Gouldner, A. W. 1961"Metaphysical Pathos and the Theory of Bureaucracy," in S. M. Lipsett and N. J. Smelser (eds.) Sociology: Progress of a Decade. Englewood Cliffs, NJ: Prentice Hall.

Graebner, Norman A., Richard Dean Burns, and Joseph M. Siracusa.Reagan, Bush, Gorbachev: revisiting the end of the Cold War. Greenwood Publishing Group, 2008: 149.

Helsinki Watch. War Crimes In Bosnia. (Human Rights Watch: USA, 1994)

Hockenos, Paul. Homeland Calling: Exile Patriotism & the Balkan Wars. Ithaca: Cornell University Press, 2003.

International Criminal Tribunal for the Former Yugoslavia Kunarac Trial. Findings of the Trial Chamber. United Nations. May 3, 1993 (S.25704).

Irvine, G. Cpl. "Blue Rocket Faceplant." http://www.peacekeeper.ca/stories2.html

Isakov, Yerlan. Stereotypes and Prejudice in Conflict: The Case of Bosnia and Herzegovina. Journal for the Study of Peace and Conflict. A Publication of The Wisconsin Institute for Peace and Conflict Studies (2010).

Jenkins, Palden. The story of Yugoslavia, When Nations fall Ill. Written 2003.

Joulwan, George A. & Shoemaker, Christopher C. Civilian-Military Cooperation in the Prevention of Deadly Conflict: Implementing Agreements in Bosnia and Beyond. (Carnegie Corporation: New York, 1998)

Kaufman, Joyce, R. NATO and the Former Yugoslavia: Crisis, Conflict, and the Atlantic Alliance. (Rowman & Littlefield: New York, 2002)

Keefe, Eugene [et al.] Journal of Military and Strategic Studies. Area handbook for Cyprus. Washington, D.C. : For sale by the Superintendent of Documents, U.S. Government Printing Office, 1971.

Lacan, J. 1977 Ecrits: A Selection. trans. Alan Sheridan. New York: W.W. Norton.

Mackenzie, Lewis. Peacekeeper: The Road to Sarajevo. Toronto: Douglas & McIntyre, 1993.

Magas, Branka. The Destruction of Yugoslavia. New York: Verso, 1993.

Mahmutcehatic, Rasmur. The Death of Bosnia. (The Pennsylvania University Press: University Park, Pennsylvania

Maloney, S.M. Canada and UN peacekeeping : Cold War by other means, 1945-1970. Vanwell Pub.: St. Catharines. 2002.

Martin, Paul. http://walterdorn.net/32-canadian-peacekeeping-proud-tradition-strong-future. 1985.

McNeill, Pearle, and Coulson, Meg. Women's Voices Refugee Lives, Stories from Bosnia. The Book People, NSW, Australia © 1994

Merril, Christopher. The Old Bridge. The Third Balkan War and Age of the Refugee Milkweed Editions, Minnesota, 1995.

Michael, Morgan L. ed. Classics of Moral and Political Theory, Third Edition. Indianapolis: Hackett, 2001.

Mojzes, Paul. "The Camoflauged Role of Religion." Religion and the War in Bosnia. Ed. Paul Mojzes. Atlanta: Scholars, 1998. 74 - 98.

O'Ballance, Edgar. Civil War in Bosnia, 1992 – 1994. (Macmillan: London, 1995)

Olujic, Maria. Embodiment of Terror: Gendered Violence in Peacetime and wartime in Croatia and Bosnia-Herzegovina. Department of Anthropology University of California, Berkeley.

Papadakis, Y., Peristianis, N., Welz, G. Divided Cyprus : modernity, history, and an island in conflict. Publication info: Bloomington : Indiana University Press, c2006.

Ridley, Jasper. Tito. London: Constable, 1994.

Ristanovic, Nesna Nikolic. Women, Violence and War Wartime Victimization of Refugees in the Balkans. Central European Press: Budapest, Hungary © 2000

Rodgers, Jayne. "Bosnia and Kosovo: Interpreting the gender dimensions of international intervention." Contemporary Security Policy 22.3 (2001): 183-195.

Rubboli, Massimo. "Canada, Peacekeeper to the World? Myths, Values, and Reality in." Building Liberty: Canada and World Peace, 1945-2005 11 (2005): 145.

Salick, Abdul, Derek. "Personal Recollections While Serving In Bosnia." 2003.

Salick, Abdul, Derek. "Trinidad and Tobago: Visioning a Nation of Great Hope." 2013.

Sekej, Laslo. Yugoslavia: The Process of Disintegration. Trans. Vera Vukelic. New York: Columbia University Press, 1993.

Seroka, Jim, and Pavlovic, Vukasin, eds. The Tragedy of Yugoslavia. New York: M.E. Sharpe, 1992

Seventh Report on War Crimes in the Former Yugoslavia Part II. Submission of Information VNSC Council. Retrieved from: http://www.phdn.org/archives/www.ess.uwe.ac.uk/documents/sdrpt7b.htm

Shatzmiller, Maya. Islam and Bosnia: Conflict Resolution and Foreign Policy In Multi-Ethnic States. (McGill-Queen's University Press: Montreal, 2002)

Shenk, Gerald N. "Bosnia: A Case Study in Religion and Ethnic Conflict." Religion and the War in Bosnia. Ed. Paul Mojzes. Atlanta: Scholars, 1998. 99 - 107.

Silber, Laura, & Little, Allan. The Death of Yugoslavia. (Penguin: London, 1995)

Siracusa, Joseph M. The "New" Cold War History and the Origins of the Cold War. Australian Journal of Politics and History. Vol. 47, Issue 1, Article first published online 9 OCT 2008. Wiley Online (Proquest)

Skjelsbaek, I. "The Political Psychology of Rape: Bosnia and Herzegovina." (2012)

Sloan, Elinor C. Bosnia andthe New Collective Security. (Praeger: Westport, Connecticut, 1998)

Snyder, C.S.,Gabbard, W.J., May, J.D., Zulcic, N. "On the Battleground of Women's Bodies: Mass Rape in Bosnia-Herzegovina." SAGE Publications. 2006: 185-190. doi: 10.1177/0886109905286017.

Soderlund, W.C., Briggs, E.C. The Independence of South Sudan: the Role of Mass Media in the Responsibility to Prevent. Wilfrid Laurier University Press. 2014.

Stiglmayer, Alexandra. "Mass Rape: The War Against Women in Bosnia-Herzegovina." University of Nebraska Press. Lincoln and London. 1994:85.

Sudetic, Chuck. Blood and Vengance. New York: Norton, 1998.

Sendzikas, Aldona, and Richard Cavell. "Love, Hate, and Fear in Canada's Cold War." (2005): 1162-1164.

Thompson, Mark. A Paper House. New York: Pantheon, 1992.

United States General Accounting Office. Bosnia Peace Operation: Mission, Structure, And Transition Strategy of NATO's Stabilization Force (GAO: Washington, 1998)

United States General Accounting Office. Bosnia Peace Operation: Pace of Implementing Dayton Accelerated as International Involvement Increased. (GAO: Washington, 1998)

Volkan, V.D. Cyprus War and Adaptation: a Psychoanalytic History of Two Ethnic Groups in Conflict. First edition. University Press of Virginia: Charlottesville. 1979.

Vlakji, Emil. The New Totalitarian Society and the Destruction of Yugoslavia. Toronto: Legas 1999.

Vrcan, Srdjan "The Religious Factor and the War in Bosnia and Herzegovina." Religion and the War in Bosnia. Ed. Paul Mojzes. Atlanta: Scholars, 1998. 108 - 131.

Vukcevich, Bosko S. Tito: Architect of Yugoslav Disintegration. New York: Rivercross, 1994.

Whitaker, Reginald, and Steve Hewitt. Canada and the Cold War. Lorimer, 2003: 6.

ABOUT THE AUTHOR

D.A. Salick served as an infantry soldier for the Canadian Armed Forces from 1982 – 2002. He was awarded the Queen Elizabeth II Golden Jubilee award for his service to Canada. He also received several medals for peacekeeping duties. His missions included: NATO West Germany (Cold War), (UN) Cyprus, (SFOR) Bosnia Herzegovina and Macedonia. During and after service he attended York University where he completed two honour degrees in Political Science (Pols) and International Development Studies (IDS) where he made the Dean's Honour List. While at York he was recognised for his contribution to sports by receiving the, York Spirit Cup Award. Derek also received an award from the Trinidad and Tobago consulate to Toronto for his contributions to sports in Canada. He played and coached soccer/football nationally and internationally, also he ran marathons and military ironman competitions. He founded the Multicultural Women's Organisation International in 2012, a non-profit organization which focuses on empowering young women from all cultural backgrounds through sport and education to encourage them to reach their full potential. He now focuses his time and energy with the MWO and writing novels. He published his first book, *Trinidad and Tobago, Visioning a Nation of Great Hope* in 2013.

Manufactured by Amazon.ca
Bolton, ON